Couples Communication

20 Effective Skills on How to Fix Mistakes for an Extraordinary Relationship & Marriage. A Self-Help Love Therapy to Improve Dialogue, Intimacy and Eliminate Anxious Attachment

---

[Michael Gary Question]

Text Copyright © [Michael Gary Question]

All rights reserved. No part of this guide may be reproduced in any form without permission in writing from the publisher except in the case of brief quotations embodied in critical articles or reviews.

Legal & Disclaimer

The information contained in this book and its contents is not designed to replace or take the place of any form of medical or professional advice; and is not meant to replace the need for independent medical, financial, legal or other professional advice or services, as may be required. The content and information in this book has been provided for educational and entertainment purposes only.

The content and information contained in this book has been compiled from sources deemed reliable, and it is accurate to the best of the Author's knowledge, information and belief. However, the Author cannot guarantee its accuracy and validity and cannot be held liable for any errors and/or omissions. Further, changes are periodically made to this book as and when needed. Where appropriate and/or necessary, you must consult a professional (including but not limited to your doctor, attorney, financial advisor or such other professional advisor) before using any of the suggested remedies, techniques, or information in this book.

Upon using the contents and information contained in this book, you agree to hold harmless the Author from and against any damages, costs, and expenses, including any legal fees potentially resulting from the application of any of the information provided by this book. This disclaimer applies to any loss, damages or injury caused by the use and application, whether directly or indirectly, of any advice or information presented, whether for breach of contract, tort, negligence, personal injury, criminal intent, or under any other cause of action.

You agree to accept all risks of using the information presented inside this book.

You agree that by continuing to read this book, where appropriate and/or necessary, you shall consult a professional (including but not limited to your doctor, attorney, or financial advisor or such other advisor as needed) before using any of the suggested remedies, techniques, or information in this book.

DESCRIPTION

The truth is: Effective communication between couples is very important to maintain a steady and understanding relationship. Without the skill of communication, a person will be entirely disadvantaged in an intimate relationship.

Are you in love or got recently married? Are you finding it tough to approach the person whom you have fallen in love with? Read On to get a brief idea on how to strike a conversation with them.

Without being able to express or listen or communicate with each other, the partners or couples will never be able to achieve the desired level of intimacy in their relationship. By developing communication skills the couples will be able to not only establish but also preserve a depth in their relationships.

The basic problem that lies underneath an effective communication between the couples is that none of them tries to understand the reality of statement of the other one. Communication is all about the collaboration between the two people and sharing every feeling, idea and thought.

Effective communication between partners involves the following:

- Approaching a conversation with the partner.

- Listening and talking to the partner and coming to a state of coherence with the partner.

- While communicating with the partner, there are certain negative forms of communication which everyone should be aware of.

These negative feelings contaminate the entire process of communication. There are certain techniques, which if adopted will help in breaking the barriers.

The goal of the book is simple: It is a comprehensive guide to understand how well to communicate with each other. It stresses on couple communication, love therapy and various modes of improving the dialogue.

It also focuses on improving intimacy and eliminates any kind of anxiety which might be associated.

You will also learn:

- Reasons why relationships fall apart.

- How to correct common mistakes and how to recognize them.

- Reverse Engineer Your relationship with conscious habits.

- Review your current situation with respect to where you were when things started for the first time.

- Compare notes related to your happiness and future goals, so work on it.

- Use habits to revive your love.

- 20 skills for extraordinary relationships.

- The advantages of building a conscious relationship.

- Important skills for related couples.

- Important skills for married couples.

Important skills for couples with children.

Table of Contents

Table of Contents 9

Introduction 13

Chapter 1: Reasons why relationships fall apart .. 17

Causes of conflicts between couples 19

How to deal with anger 20

Communication as a cornerstone to work on yourself 21

Physical acts 26

Chapter 2: How to correct common mistakes and how to recognize them 29

Chapter 3: Reverse Engineer Your relationship with conscious habits 42

- Review your current situation with respect to where you were when things started for the first time 44

- Compare notes related to your happiness and future goals, so work on it 49

Chapter 4: Use habits to revive your love 55

Chapter 5: 20 skills for extraordinary relationships 68

.... 68

1: Abandoning Your Ego 68
2: How to Build Healthy Habits as A Couple 70
3: Developing Emotional Intelligence 72
4: Developing Empathy Listening 74
5: Don't Be Afraid to Show Weakness 76
6: Understanding Body Language 78
.... 80
7: Learning to Talk About It 80
8: Digitally Disconnecting 82
9: Apologizing Mindfully 83
10: No Judgment Zone 85
11: Working on Yourself First 87
12: Using Irony to Diffuse Unpleasant Situations 89
13: A Couple That Laughs Together, Stays Together 91
14: Don't Neglect the Sexual Aspect 94
15: Getting Some Space 96
16: Setting Goals Together 99
17: Don't' Hold onto Anger 101
18: Sincerity Matters 103
19: Productive Conflict Helps 105
20: Developing Diplomatic Dialogue Skills 107

Chapter 6: The advantages of building a conscious relationship 111

- Important skills for related couples 112

- Important skills for married couples 119

- Important skills for couples with children 127

Chapter 7: How to deal with serious problems 134

- Some useful exercises and examples 135

    Communication exercises + games 141

- Pointers and in-depth information in an informative and friendly way, ... 145

Chapter 8: improving dialogue, intimacy and eliminating anxious attachment 155

- Improves dialogue 156

- Improves intimacy 161

- Eliminates anxious attachment 181

Chapter 9: Couple communication. Love therapy. 203

- Facilitate communication 206

- Get past discussions on major issues 210

Conclusion 214

Introduction

It is likely that you have heard of the importance of communication in marriage many times over since you first got together with your spouse. Still, knowing the importance of communication and knowing how to apply strong communication skills to a marriage are two completely different things. While many people love to educate us on the importance of communicating with our partners, few ever actually tell us how. Fortunately for you, I am going to outline the importance of communication in marriages and exactly how you can begin communicating with your spouse in a strong way.

Knowing how to communicate effectively requires you to have the information around what effective communication is; a clear understanding of how to apply it, and a great deal of practice. Most times, poor communication skills are a result of bad habits and simply not knowing any better. It is rare that a person truly intends to communicate poorly with their spouse, or anyone else. After all, knowing the negative impact that poor communication can have on a relationship is reason enough to want to do better. That being said, practicing effective communication will require you to both learn new habits and break old ones.

Because you are looking to communicate better specifically with your spouse, it can be beneficial for you to read this book together with your spouse. When you are both working on these techniques together, it is easier for you both to have compassion for each other and patience for the lessons that you are learning together. It is also a good way to remind each other to practice better communication skills if you notice that your partner is practicing an old bad habit.

Furthermore, learning new things and growing together with your partner is a wonderful way to increase intimacy in your relationship. This happens by developing a layer of respect, which creates a sense of safety, which builds a feeling of trust, which nurtures the evolution of intimacy. When you spend time focusing on these four aspects together, as you will throughout this book, it is easier to improve the quality of your marriage in a way that is sustainable and lasting.

Communicating in your marriage is not always going to be easy. It is likely that if you are reading this book that your communication may have already reached a noticeable state of trouble. As a result, you may have healing that needs to be done in addition to improved communication. In this case, make sure that you are extra patient with each other and that you incorporate the healing that needs to be done into learning how to communicate with each other. This will support you both in healing the pain and creating a resolution that will help you prevent future hurt from taking root in your relationship.

Another reason why you may struggle with communication is that of the very intimacy that you share with your partner. Telling them about difficult or vulnerable pieces of information or dealing with conflict in a marriage can be challenging. Knowing how to deal with these more challenging parts of communication effectively can ensure that your difficult conversations end on a positive note. As a result, you and your spouse will end up feeling even closer to each other.

Chapter 1: Reasons why relationships fall apart

mImage 1: Free Credits

The couple is made of two people; both must be responsible for their balance first. Change yourself to the better if you want to help your partner to be a better person.

Everybody gets angry for one reason or the other. Whether it shows or not, we are all bound to feeling tension when people overstep their boundaries, or certain matters go wrong. In marriages, spouses can avoid showing anger to avoid conflict. They shove it down and let it go unnoticed.

However, hidden anger is just as bad as that which explodes because, at one point or the other, it will hurt the relationship. In most cases, the more one lets the arguments to go on, the more the distance between him/her and the partner grows. The longer it lasts, the harder it is for the couple to repair the relationship and at such points, people look for divorce papers.

As human beings, anger pushes us to say or do things that WE would not do in normal circumstances. We should remember that once words are said and actions are done, it is impossible to unsay or undo them. When we explode, we should be careful about how we deal with anger. The emotion of anger is not right or wrong by itself. The morality of emotions and feelings comes in question only when we react to what we are feeling. For example, feeling angry is okay but destroying things out of anger brings the morality aspect.

Causes of conflicts between couples

More often than not, human beings forget that they are different and that each has a different opinion and view of things. This happens a lot in marriage because the love and attraction make the couple feel like they are one. Although marriage brings 'two people together to become one' their minds still differ, their backgrounds are different, their upbringing is different; therefore they cannot have the same opinions all the time.

Everyone has a different memory and perception, and there is no one right and standard way of thinking. Even when you know that your opinion is right, your line of thought and perspective is not the only right one. A couple consists of two people, and if it is only one person who keeps giving their opinion without considering the opinion of the other one, then the marriage is made up on one person. This means that there is no room in the marriage for the two people and thus the communication stops, and the marriage no longer functions properly.

There are many different ways of dealing with issues positively without having fights that will end up destroying the communication. Spouses do not have to strive to fix each other rather; they should look for ways to agree and disagree positively. A couple should constantly deal with unresolved anger and issues. Do not bottle up things, feelings, emotions, opinions et cetera even if it is for the sake of the other person. Letting thing go without sorting them out fast and soon only leads to deeper conflicts and more distance to the extent of everyone using a confrontational tone and attitude even when they should not.

How to deal with anger

Firstly, when a spouse is wrong, he/she should not hesitate to apologize. Words such as 'I am sorry' go a long way in making a partner reconsider their next words. When honesty is applied by the person apologizing, there is no more room for more arguments. Conceding defeat does not make one weak and apologizing helps to loosen tension which might have escalated to disconnection and complete lack of communication. Staying stubborn and trying to 'fix' a partner will not help solve anything. Standing a ground is only necessary when the couple will win together but if the victory belongs to one person, chances are a brick wall will grow between them. It is therefore important that everybody communicates effectively, practice saying the right things to each other, build one another, talk to each other and avoid talking at one another.

Communication as a cornerstone to work on yourself

If one were to go to a crowd of people and ask them to name the most important aspect of marriage, they would mention a variety of things including trust, honesty love et cetera. Every person has their understanding of love and marriage, and they have their preferences. Of course, all the aspects that the people would mention play a crucial role in marriages but communication is the centerpiece of all communication.

The way the two spouses communicate with each other, discuss their issues, encourage and build one another through communication is essential for the sustainment of a fulfilling marriage. One can say that communication is the vehicle that carries all the other aspects of marriage. Without communication, that is verbal and verbal; a spouse could not know whether to trust and be honest with their partners. Assumptions usually break the marriage. If one person loves the other and does not talk about it or at least show it in words, they will not succeed in marriage. To the spouses; if you love your partner, let them know through words and actions.

If the communication between two people is honest, then the chances of the relationship surviving are high. Communication is the cornerstone of all relationship; however, many people are not good at communicating. Other people do not know how to address matters in the right way. Spouses need to use certain communication channels to create a strong and caring atmosphere in their marriage. Love, honesty trust and other important parts of marriage are not meaningful by themselves. One must be able to express these aspects to give them meaning. The expression of love and care in marriage is what makes it worth envy. Showing love acting honestly and showcasing trust is where the magic of marriage lies. The ability to communicate with a spouse about how much they mean to each other is where a marriage graduates from good to great. One should remember that communication is more than speaking about things; it is also showing. Under the umbrella of communication between couples, we can identify verbal, non-verbal and physical acts.

Verbal communication between couples

Verbal communication is the easiest and most commonly used form of communication. Words are easy to use to a large extent. People like to hear things especially when they are nice. For instance, every spouse loves to be complemented through words 'you look very nice today,' 'I love you.' You are a great person with an amazing personality.' Effective communication requires one to be able to express their feelings to their spouse through words. If a couple loves each other so much yet they are unable to communicate the same through words; they might never know how much they mean to each other. Even when the actions show clearly that the spouses love one another, they still need to say it in words. Words will add value to the actions and vice versa. They will make the involved parties feel appreciated, loved, and sure about how the other person feels.

Along with all the compliments and expression of the positive, the spouses can express what they are not happy about through words. If a spouse is doing something that is offending the other, yet the offended person is silent about it, the offender will most probably continue with their habits. Silence does not help in most cases. If anything, lack of communication will keep hurting the couple. One cannot possibly go through life while holding all the dissatisfaction inside. Verbal communication will help one let it all out. However, when letting matters out, one should be tactful and careful. Care and warmth in communication are essential, especially when talking about matters that might bring disagreements. Couples should not wait too long before they say something about things bothering them. They should also not wait too long before telling each other that they care.

Nonverbal communication between couples

At some point in life, we have said something unpleasant or unfriendly to someone else. They might not have retaliated verbally, but they show their displeasure through facial expressions and actions either voluntarily or involuntarily. The offended person did not have to say a word to tell the story, but it all showed on their faces. Human beings share more with their faces and body than they would give credit.

Spouses should be aware of their facial expression and body language while talking to their partners to avoid giving off the wrong message. Human beings are capable of reading the body language of their partners even subconsciously. If for example, a couple is having a serious conversation and one person id hunched over and probably closed off, the other will detect a lack of vulnerability. Use the right facial and body language for every conversation. For example, if a couple s having a serious conversation, it is important that the two parties

Face each other and keep their body language open without crossing the legs or arms. The body language should show that the person is listening keenly, taking note of the important things and is willing to work through the subject matter. Nonverbal cues are many, and they communicate to the partner either positively or negatively even without an exchange of words. Everyone should be conscious and thoughtful of how their body language brings out their thoughts.

Physical acts

Physical acts include making dinner, doing the laundry, taking out the garbage, and even getting ice-cream from the fridge for a pregnant wife. Physical actions are not things one can express through words. They are things that one does for their spouses to show them how much they care. IN DOING SUCH simple things, one is communicating with their partners about how much they mean to them without using words. This form of communication falls under the phrase "Actions speak louder than words." You could sing your spouse that you love them till your face turns blue, but it would not mean as much as making him/her dinner or replacing their old attire. The power of actions outdoes the power of saying I love you 300 times a day.

Having in mind that communication is important for the success of marriage; one cannot rely on just one of the ways mentioned above. Every spouse should strike a balance between the three to ensure that the marriage thrives. It is okay for a spouse to tell their partner that they love them and at the same time give an opinion about things that are bothering them. Open communication will benefit the marriage in the long term and become an investment to reap from. Every person should use body language to show their spouses that they are honest and open with them. An observant eye will pick negative body language no matter how well one hides it. A spouse may take this as a red flag for the beginning of the end of the marriage. Couples need to stay alert about what they communicate through their bodies and make appropriate adjustments so that the spouse can read honesty and trust

Again, a couple should use actions to communicate to their spouses A gift or two, a body massage, a dinner date, or even assisting with a troubling task can go a long way to communicate to each other. Actions will always speak for themselves; even if one was to keep singing that they love someone yet they fail to show it in actions, then they will fail. Without open and effective communication, a couple will face more challenges and obstacles than otherwise.

Chapter 2: How to correct common mistakes and how to recognize them

Image 2: Free Credits

Who doesn't enjoy the feeling of being in a budding relationship? The fresh flush of love, being wooed and swept off the feet by your potential make! The feel good endorphin rush in the brain that keeps you happy, driven and positive all the time! For many people, this is the most perfect phase of a relationship, which only goes downhill from here. Well, not really. The relationship can solidify and get even stronger if you communicate effectively during the initial stages.

Here are some of the best communication tips for a budding romantic relationship

1. Own Past Mistakes

Work your way through past mistakes and disappointments rather than pretending they didn't exist. If something went wrong in the past relationship owing to your mistake, accept it to avoid repeating it in the current relationship or you're going down heartbreak alley all over again.

For example, if you pretended to be something you were not in a bid to put your best foot forward and impress your date, which was later discovered and the relationship ended on a sour note, be genuine this time. Reveal your real, genuine, honest self to the other person in an attempt to undo or mend past relationship mistakes. Own it or accept responsibility for past mistakes and move ahead. If you have the option of seeing a therapist or attending an assistance program, consider opting for it to overcome past issues and start the new relationship on a fresh slate. Clear the cob webs, clear your feelings and begin on a more positive note.

2. Acquire Skills Gradually

The truth is you will learn certain communication patterns only over a period of time by communicating more and more with the person. This means you'll need to invest time in listening to your partner, understanding them, knowing what they like or dislike, their views about major things in life.

Make it your main objective to understand them. Take time out to actively listen to them. Put your ego and need to be right all the time aside. Your primary intention should be to understand the person and be understood. Rather than constructing your own clever responses, focus on what your partner is trying to convey.

3. Avoid Bringing the Past Into The Present

We are often tempted to bring out past into the present through a series of assumptions and comparisons. Sometimes, unknowingly, you may carry the anger, frustration or hurt of a previous relationship into a new relationship, which is grossly unfair to the new partner. You may not have done the groundwork to overcome the pitfall of the former relationship, the price of which may be your current relationship.

Avoid making assumptions based on past relationships by not listening carefully to your partner. He/she may be trying to communicate something totally different than what you assume using your past relationship filters. Give them time, space and confidence to speak by listening to them and more importantly, understanding them correctly.

Constantly interrupting them or dishing off their feelings/emotions as unfounded or invalid can prove disastrous. Don't make sweeping statements such as "you never …. "or "you always." Keep it thoughtful and unfiltered. For a while just listen to them without trying to judge them. The trouble in budding relationships is we quickly try to compare and judge potential partners rather than attempting to understand them. Observe them with more understanding tinted glasses, and communication will flow.

4. Avoid Oversharing

I know people who in a bid to prove to their partner that they are really serious about the relationship end up sharing much more than they should. They think it makes them come across as human, vulnerable and endearing. Of course, honesty and openness are appreciated in any relationship. However, there is a right time for sharing everything. You don't have to plunge into the relationship head on and reveal your deepest, darkest and unknown secrets to your new partner.

Since they are also getting to know you and may not understand the secrets in their right context, you run the risk of creeping them out and ending the relationship. Give them time to know and understand you to view your secrets in the right context. In a situation where they don't have any previous information to go by, there is a high chance that they may not understand what you are trying to communicate.

When we meet people for the first time or for a couple of times, the information we get is generally overemphasized because we don't know any better. There is no foundation or basis against which we can view what a new partner just communicated. When you share personal and deep secrets, the other person will give these details more significance than needed.

On the other hand, when you spend more time with a person in the long haul, you have a larger context to view what they've just stated. Their quirks, actions, thoughts and behaviors can be viewed in the correct light.

Of course, you want to share more intimate or vulnerable details about yourself to reveal your trust in the other person. So what's the middle way? Allow yourself to be occasionally vulnerable when the mood is perfect or you find your partner sharing vulnerable details too.

However, don't make it too revealing a conversation prematurely. If at all you end up sharing more than required, admit that you are feeling slightly insecure about whatever you've told them. Their reaction will help you determine if they display understanding towards what you've shared. This can be your clue to sharing or not sharing more in the future (if there is a future after what you've shared that is lol).

5. Don't Come On Too Strong For Heaven's Sake

Don't come across as too available or eager to jump into the relationship through your verbal and non-verbal communication. The partner will wonder whether you want to be in a relationship with them or you are simply desperate to be in a relationship, even with a wall. It doesn't really tell the other person that you love or adore them.

Though it may seem overhyped, there is some element of truth in the notion that we crave something we can't easily have even more. If you appear desperate and go all out to please your partner by making yourself too available or too in their face all the time, you may not be doing it right. We strive harder for rewards that appear beyond our reach. Coming on too strongly can be a terrible turn-off for your partner. It will make them lose interest, and they'll communicate with you in a more disinterested manner. People will fast lose interest if you come across as too overbearing.

Also, you'd like to spend more time together with your partner to understand them without coming across as too eager. Talk to them and set expectations right in the beginning to ensure you both are aligned in the same direction. Determine how often you want to meet or how much time you wish to spend together. Once expectations are clarified, there is little room for disappointment, miscommunication and frustration.

6. Pray Don't Be Dismissive

This is another extreme of the above point. Sometimes, in their need to come across as more desirable or irresistible, people purposefully limit or restrict communication with their budding partners. It is the subtle art of showing people we really don't care. Don't be available all the time but don't cut off someone to establish your importance or superiority. Some people assume that they'll know instantly whether there's a connection with the other person. Guess what? It may not always be true. At times, you just need to give it more time to understand that the other person is perfect for you. There may not be a Eureka or ringing bells, falling flowers moment. You may need weeks to determine if the relationship will work.

Don't dismiss a potential partner or budding relationship simply because you didn't feel it right in the beginning or even after a few days. Understand that relationships need time to nurture, which can be done through communication and understanding. Just because it doesn't feel right or perfect in the beginning doesn't mean it isn't meant to be. The best of relationships can grow and thrive over a period of time if nurtured with love, communication and understanding.

It happens on television shows and movies but real life is different! I know several mediocre or even downright disastrous first dates that transformed into awesome relationships only because the people involved gave it another chance. Give the person more time before dismissing him or her.

7. Revealing Insecurity

If you ask me to mention my number one relationship killer in the early days, it is revealing your insecurity. When you start dating someone, there is plenty of grey area, along with uncertainties and assumptions. If you have any genuine concerns, talk it out with your partner. However, it isn't fair to make your new partner the target of your insecurities, when they don't deserve it. Try to get to the bottom of your feelings.

Where have your feelings originated from? Why do you feel the way you feel? Was an earlier relationship or person responsible for making you feel the way you do? Did an incident or occurrence in a previous relationship ruin things for you? Has your previous partner been unfaithful to you? Don't allow jealousy or insecurity to determine how you treat the other person. Instead, address the root cause of the issue. You can deal with it on your own and enlist your partner's help too.

Speak to them in a frank, open and candid manner about how you feel. Tell them you don't want to come across as insecure or jealous but a few incidents or past relationships have turned you into a more insecure person, and that you are genuinely working on it. You can also tell them how you need their help in the process.

Sometimes, it is great to witness some mistakes early in the relationship because they offer some realistic or practical tests for couples. Do you communicate effectively as a couple? Are you as a couple apologetic or accusatory? These are all indicators which will help you lay the foundation of a healthy relationship.

Don't fret if you just started seeing someone and hit a slight roadblock. Work through your couple mistakes. Even if you make a mistake, view it as an opportunity to grow together instead of giving up even without trying and throwing away a relationship which could have been wonderful in the long run.

8. Don't Get Defensive

When we open up to a new relationship, the temptation to jump to our own defensive is pretty high. If a new mate challenges something you say or do, you want to prove to them that you are right so they don't view you in a negative light. However, being defensive doesn't always help. On the contrary, you'll come across as egoistic, dogmatic and self-centered. Position yourself as someone who is open to hearing different perspectives and points of view.

Demonstrate your ability to listen, appreciate and understand your new partner's perspective even if you don't necessarily believe in it. Be open to discussions and listen calmly to the other person's perspective. Own up to your thoughts or actions rather than defending them and making a fool of yourself. If the person doesn't accept you, trust me, you are much better off without them.

Learn the subtle art of communicating without getting defensive. This is even truer in a relatively budding relationship. Build a foundation for a mutually respectful and loving relationship. Even if you don't agree about some things, don't attack or misjudge the other person.

Chapter 3: Reverse Engineer Your relationship with conscious habits

IImage 3: Free Credits

Listening is vital in creating proper dialogue, which in turn is essential to maintaining a healthy relationship. When there's a communication breakdown there's always a chance for misunderstandings and confusion that can lead to bitterness, or the development of overall poor communication between you.

Without open lines of communication with our partner, they can feel unsupported, unappreciated, and even unwanted. Relationships that want to last are built on honesty, openness, trust, and mutual respect. Building a productive, supportive, and caring relationship is only possible if we develop effective communication skills.

Communication is a two-way street and include compromise. We have to be able to honestly voice our feelings because keeping things bottled-up can foster malcontent and can even be detrimental to our overall health. When we focus on listening to our significant other, and they listen to us, it is less likely that there will be misunderstandings.

We all tend to 'vent' sometimes and of course, there are times when that is indeed necessary and even therapeutic. But if there is an issue that seriously needs to be addressed and resolved and we simply go on a mad rant instead of discussing it calmly, chances are high that our partner will just think we are just blowing off steam and may well just tune us out. Get those rants out when necessary but remember the items we've discussed so far and strive to convey your grievance clearly. Without it sounding like it's something you just need to 'get off your chest.'

When we feel that we have really been listened to, and not just 'heard,' it helps us validate that our partner does value our opinion and feelings. Thinking that we're underappreciated or not respected doesn't work at school or at our jobs and it certainly won't work in a relationship – not one that has any hope of lasting long-term.

When we are properly communicating, then our focus is on each other and nothing else. This always helps bring us closer together and helps ensure a healthy relationship.

- **Review your current situation with respect to where you were when things started for the first time**

Talking about serious issues is a critical part of communication in a marriage. You should be able to let your partner know what you feel or think without disrupting your bond. How you deliver your message and how you carry out the discussion matters. Only a healthy discussion about serious issues can be fruitful. The following are some ways to effectively address serious issues within your marriage.

Find a good time.

Starting the discussion on serious issues at the right time is essential. When you pick a good time, you can communicate better. Discussing serious issues after dinner is a good choice. Don't have serious discussions too early in the morning or just before you sleep. If there is chaos around you or everyone seems too busy, just wait for a better time to talk.

Think before you speak.

It's important that you weigh the effect of your words on your partner before you utter them. Do not say insensitive things, make sarcastic remarks, be negative or play the blame game during the conversation. Be soft, tender and tell your partner exactly how you feel without the tinges of negativity in your words. They think about you too so keep that in mind.

Deal with important issues early.

Some important issues which affect the entire family should be addressed before things get out of hand. Avoid escalating the matter and try to discuss it intellectually beforehand. Make sure you have a solid discussion when the time is right.

Keep everything private.

This point has a double meaning. Keep your conversation between you two and do not let a third person into your issues. This only causes external interference and usually ends up paving a rocky path for both of you. Secondly, be sure that you do not compare your family with other families during your conversation. You can always find an example of another family doing something, and comparing is simply not fair.

Explore your spouse's beliefs, thoughts and feelings.

Your spouse feels various emotions and has different thoughts and beliefs compared to you. Respect their ways of thinking and emotions. Look deeply into their heart. Put yourself in their shoes and make empathy your strength. Make it your priority to respect their opinions. Give your spouse a full chance to say what they want to say. Do not make the mistake of being judgmental about your spouse's opinions and beliefs. This can create friction between the two of you and raise a communication barrier. Make eye contact and be attentive while listening to your partner so they feel encouraged to be more open to you. Stay open-minded.

Prepare to receive a defensive or negative response.

Of course, disagreements and arguments do occur during a conversation between partners. This is a sign of a healthy and active participation in a conversation. Don't expect your partner to agree with everything you say. Your spouse will give you a negative response at times. They may get defensive and try to argue over some points. Be calm during that time and let your spouse speak. Listen to them but try to make your point clear. Your spouse will get it after some time or after a series of conversations. Soon enough, your spouse will realize they had been wrong. That is, if it was really your spouse who had been wrong to begin with.

Tailor the message.

Your message should be very simple in its essence. Tailor the message according to the recipient's mind and their background. Make it simple, short and to the point. Avoid beating about the bush and choose the most appropriate opening lines for the conversation. Be direct in your words and be rational despite the storm of emotions building up inside you. Take a logical road to get a better outcome from the discussion. It needs to have a positive effect on your family. Don't be boring. Use simple language and avoid using heavy vocabulary. This isn't a formal discussion. You are trying to find solutions for a better future.

Be honest.

Make sure you are honest about your feelings. Your spouse will automatically feel obliged to be attentive towards your emotions when they sense your sincerity. Give your spouse a chance to set things right and make amendments for their mistakes. Tell your husband or wife what's bothering you. Show that you are hurt by their actions but also let your spouse feel that you are forgiving as well. Your partner will certainly realize their mistake and avoid hurting you with such an action in the future.

- **Compare notes related to your happiness and future goals, so work on it**

How many times have you looked on with envy at other happy couples whom you know? Or even the happy couples that you randomly see around you gazing lovingly into each other's eyes or holding hands as they stroll through the park? They seem almost picture perfect, don't they? But of course, every relationship comes with its own challenges. These happy couples have just found a way to work through those challenges together by communicating well and relying on each other for support. That's the secret to their success.

Now, working on building a lasting relationship is not going to be easy. You can't just enter into a relationship and hope for the best - or that your problems are going to sort themselves out. In fact, the **Public Discourse** published an article in 2015 which revealed that at least 40-50% of marriages tend to end in divorce. Researchers who spend their time analyzing relationships have always been motivated to find the qualities and traits which contribute to the happiness of a relationship, and one of these factors is to start building happy relationships as a couple.

Healthy Habits That Happy Couples Engage In

Building a happy, healthy relationship starts with building healthy habits together as a couple. Which is why this is Skill #2 that you're about to learn. Why do we need to actively work on building healthy habits? Because in a 2013 **Journal of Social and Personal Relationships** publication by Ogolsky and Bowers, research supported the idea that those who put in the effort to work on their relationships were the ones who managed to cultivate relationships with lasting happiness.

There are healthy habits which happy couples regularly engage in, and here are some practices you can begin applying in your own relationship to improve how you communicate with your partner or spouse:

• **Always Express Your Appreciation -** Do it all day, every day because you can never express appreciation enough. It is always better that your partner feels the extra love and appreciation that you feel for them instead of feeling underappreciated. Love the little things that they do? Let them know! You don't have to do anything elaborate, just simple little gestures, thank you notes, even text messages sent throughout the day letting them know how much you appreciate them can make a huge difference in someone's day.

• **Ask, And You Shall Receive -** Another healthy habit that a lot of couples tend to ignore is to just ask for what they want. Don't assume your partner is going to pick up on the little hints or read your mind and know how to anticipate your thoughts. Assumption is where a lot of communication breakdown tends to happen, which then escalates into fights that could have been avoided. If you want your partner to do something, don't be afraid to just **ask** for it.

• **Working on Chores Together** - This is easily one habit that can be done together, so one person doesn't feel the burden of having to upkeep the house all by themselves. In fact, dividing the workload promotes great teamwork and a sense of happiness knowing that you can count on your partner to share in the workload with you. Rotate the chores amongst yourselves, so there's a sense of fairness and balance, and one person is not stuck doing the same thing all the time.

• **They Can Move On** - The biggest downfall in any relationship is the inability of one partner to let things go and move on. Sometimes perhaps both partners could have the tendency to hold onto grudges and bring up issues of the past in arguments. It is time to start cultivating the habit of letting this go. When you have a disagreement or an argument about something, work it out, apologize if need be, and then move on. Let that be the end of it. Forget about it and don't bring it up again in future arguments. It can be a difficult habit to start practicing and adopting in the beginning, but it is a habit that is going to make a huge difference in your relationship once you do.

- **Be Respectful Towards Each Other -** Couples that don't respect each other will have a much harder time staying together. Respect is a vital habit towards cultivating the happiness in your relationship that you seek. Each time that you show disrespect towards your partner, you are in a way letting them know that you don't accept them for the way that they are. Remember that your partner is a unique individual, just like you are, and part of being in a relationship is accepting others and valuing them for who they are, not who you expect them to be.

- **Indulge in Common Interests Activities -** Spend some time doing activities together that **both** you and your partner enjoy. There are bound to be some things that you have in common. It could be a hobby, sport or activity that you like to do together, a shared passion over food perhaps, or even a favorite TV show that both of you love. Make it a habit to do these things together as a couple, it can be great for enhancing your communication skills, especially for activities where you need to work together as a team.

- **Hugging Hello and Goodbye -** When you leave for work in the mornings, start making it a habit to hug your partner and tell them you love them before you head out the door (if you're not doing it already). Wish them a great day ahead, give them a kiss and a hug and those little habits can have a tremendous effect on how both of you feel. It's a great way to start the day on a positive note. When you come home from work in the evenings, greet each other again with a hug and a kiss, asking them how their day was and let them know that you missed them. You could even make this habit something that you do each time you leave or come home, even if it is for little things like running errands or going out to catch up with a few friends for a drink.

Chapter 4: Use habits to revive your love

Image 4: Credits Kim Magnago Photo

So you are sure that you've found the best possible partner ever and wish to take your relationship to its next phase? Or maybe your partner wants marriage and you're not yet ready. How can you communicate this to your partner without hurting? How do you tell them that you need more time without inconsiderate or insensitive? How do you raise the topic of marriage without appearing pushy?

If you've been going around for a while, it is natural to think that it is time to take the relationship ahead. You want to pop the big question, but you are also unsure about your partner's reaction. Or maybe you are caught off guard after your partner pops the marriage question. There are several questions in your mind, including where is the relationship headed? Is it a long term relationship? Is your partner truly the "one?"

Do you imagine yourself spending the rest of your life with him or her? You are serious with a person and wondering how to make things move ahead with them. How do you raise the topic of marriage? The most important thing is to match your goals and intentions in the long run.

Here are some tips for discussing marriage or taking your relationship serious.

1. Be Straightforward

When you are talking about taking your relationship to the next level or suggesting marriage, keep it simple and straightforward. All the same, make your conversation low pressure. You can say something such as, "I know I want to get married in future. How do you feel about the same? You are keeping it open-ended and non-accusatory and aren't accompanying the idea by pressure.

Avoid statements such as, "Are you ever going to get married?" or "Are you planning to marry me before I die?" or "what are we really?" Approach this topic pretty much like other challenging and tricky topics with loads of maturity and positivity. You and your partner may not necessarily be on the same page when it comes to a topic as sensitive as marriage. He or she may just not be ready. You should respect that instead of putting pressure on them and making them feel miserable about their choice.

When a person says "not now" or "they aren't ready yet," it doesn't mean never. It just means they need more time. Give them the time and space to sort out their priorities and responsibilities.

2. Use a General and Gentle Approach

If you get freaked out trying a straightforward or pointed approach, use a general conversation approach. Say, for example, you have a friend who got married recently. Very smoothly yet casually draw this into a conversation with your partner. If nothing, you'll be able to determine their interest in getting married or at least know their views on marriage. This moves works especially well if you have a slight hint that your partner may have negative views or feelings about marriage, and you wish to avoid a potentially awkward and disappointing forthright conversation.

Approach the conversation slowly and gently. Frame your expectation as a question and not a high pressure expectation. For instance, ask "How do you view the future of our bond or relationship?" or "Have you considered marriage down the line?" It sounds non-threatening.

3. Ditch The Ultimatums

Irrespective of how you broach the topic of marriage, avoid issuing ultimatums to your partner to manipulate them into doing what you want. Yes, however frustrated you are, issuing ultimatums is akin to subtly manipulating the person into giving in to your demands. We've all done it at some point or the other in a relationship.

The underlying idea is, you really don't want to force yourself or the idea of commitment on someone isn't really keen on taking it ahead yet. Why should you have to convince someone about marrying you? Isn't it counterproductive? People should want to be with you on their own. If they don't, give them more time. There's no point selling yourself or the idea of marriage to someone who clearly doesn't feel it on their own. Honestly, I would never want to convince someone to marry me! Proposals backed by threat are the worst. They push a person in the opposite direction and make them feel like their view or opinion is not important.

4. Don't Make Assumptions

Alright, you both love traveling, playing golf and gorging on desserts. That doesn't mean you are on the same page when it comes to marriage. Don't automatically assume that because you have similar interests or likes, you both are destined to get married. You may not be on a similar page where commitment or marriage is concerned.

I also know of instances when couples start dating wanting marriage and then don't really feel the same way one year into the relationship, which is alright. When it comes to taking your relationship ahead or committing into a bond, talk to your partner. Instead of sitting and assuming things, have a real conversation with him or her to understand their hopes, expectations, fears and concerns.

Do not assume that you are invariably headed in the direction of the altar simply on the basis that you both love each other.

5. Listen Keenly

Listen to what your partner is saying. Read between the lines to understand the underlying feelings and intentions. Sometimes, your direct approach may catch them off-guard. They may something you really don't want to hear. Encourage them to express themselves honestly.

There are several reasons why people may be averse to the idea of marriage or commitment, including personal insecurities, bitter relationships or marriages in the past, childhood experiences related to their parents' bitter relationship, perceived loss of freedom, greater responsibilities and much more. Listen to the other person to understand their concerns. Even if you both want marriage, your reasons can be completely different.

For example, your partner may want marriage for practical and financial reasons since it makes sense to run a single home than two. On the other hand, your partner may want to get married because they want someone to come back and talk to. Your reasons may be practical, while your partners may be more romantic.

When you talk frankly and honestly about the idea of marriage and commitment, you'll discover diverse perspectives and expectations. Of course, if you are bringing up the subject if marriage, you will be speaking more in the beginning. However, once you realize that the other person is replying to your questions, listen. When you direct the conversation, you are preventing your partner from sharing their truest feelings. Instead of speaking honestly, they will most likely tell you what you want to hear.

The same is true for hearing something you may not like. Listen carefully to their reasoning. For example, a person may really want to marry you but they may want to be more financially secure before they take the plunge. He or she may want to get their house in place first before marrying you. If you finish the conversation without letting him/her share, you may start believing that they don't want to marry you at all, which is not the truth at all.

Eliminate the scope for misunderstanding by listening keenly to what the person is saying.

6. Take a Stock of Your Motives

Before you begin talking about marriage with your partner, understand your motives for getting or not getting married. Why do you want to get married or not get married? Is it for financial or personal security? Is it owing to tradition? Do you want to get married to have children? Have a good grip on your motives, intentions and desires for getting married?

This will help you have a more thoughtful or meaningful conversation with your partner. It also offers greater insight into the other person about what your underlying motives are to make a decision. Whether he or she agrees to what you are saying or gives in to your demand largely depends on your underlying motives, and how you communicate it to your partner.

7. Don't Try To Be Too Cool

We are all guilty of making this mistake, where we pretend we don't really care when we really want something to happen. You know the drill, right? You act all cool and like you don't give a damn just to save yourself the hurt and disappointment. If these things aren't really important to you, it is all good.

However, it isn't cool to pretend to have priorities that are different from your actual priorities. It isn't really fair for either you or your partner. Honestly is the best approach when it comes to talking about marriage and commitment.

8. Don't Rush If You Don't Want To

Yes, marriage is a huge decision. Career wise, financially and personally! You may have legitimate reasons for not being ready for marriage yet. You may not want additional responsibility of your shoulder yet when you are still trying to find your bearings in a new job or career. Similarly, you may not be in a position to devote time to having and raring children if you are on the brink of your career.

You'll have to feel with your heart, but you'll also have to use your mind for thinking rationally about a life changing decision. Do not let your partner put you under any pressure or manipulate you into giving in to their demand. There are plenty of energy drainers in our life to add more. Don't rush. Communicate with your partner gently and assertively that you need more time. Tell them that you adore them and that it isn't about them but how you feel unprepared or need more time to come to terms with a bigger commitment. Don't focus on them; make it about your lack of readiness. At the same time, ensure they know that "not now" doesn't mean "never."

Ask your partner questions such as, "Why do you want to get married?" " Why do you want to make it happen so quickly?" "What do we gain from the marriage that we don't have already?" and other similar questions. Ask yourself if you are truly willing to spend your life with a person who is pressurizing you into making such an important issue about your life. Doesn't it reflect unflatteringly on them if they are pushing you into making a decision? This may just be a teaser or trailer of things to follow. Even if your partner doesn't agree with you, he/she must respect your feelings and choices.

9. Be True to Yourself

Whether you want marriage or not, learn to be true to yourself. Don't go with something just because your partner is saying it or you feel compelled to agree with them. You have your own independent feelings and opinions, which should be expressed in a healthy, polite and assertive manner. Express your honest feelings about marriage. Is marriage a priority for you in the immediate future? Are you on the same thought process or plane as your partner? Don't pretend you are if you aren't.

Validate their feelings. I am not advocating dismissing what the other person wants. However, don't feel the need to conform to what he/she is saying just to make him/her happy. For instance, if you partner wants to get married and you don't, you can say something like, "I really value my relationship with you. However, marriage is a huge commitment and shift in priorities. I'd appreciate if you would give me more time to figure it out or think about it."

Your partner's reaction can speak volumes about how much they respect your wishes. This conversation can either award a new lease to your relationship or be the cause of discord.

Chapter 5: 20 skills for extraordinary relationships

IImage 5: Free Credits

1: Abandoning Your Ego

A loving relationship. That's what we all want. That's what we all desire.

But anyone who has ever been - or is currently- in a relationship will tell you that happy, loving, and healthy relationships are not something that happens just like that. It takes hard work and for both parties to be equally invested and committed enough to put in the effort to **want to build** this relationship.

According to psychologist K. Daniel O'Leary back in 2012 when he and his research team conducted a study into long-term marriages, what was interesting was that happy couples were the ones who both endorsed and expressed the positive feelings that they had for their partners or spouses. The study revealed that 40% of the couples who have been married for more than 10 years affirmed that they were still very much in love.

Signs Your Ego Is Damaging Your Relationship

If you're wondering whether ego is playing a part in preventing effective communication from taking place with your partner, take a look at the following signs:

- You're constantly blaming your partner for everything, without taking any responsibility for your actions. It is always someone else's fault.

- You find yourself playing the "victim card" far too often in your relationship.

- You get jealous easily, which leads to a lot of arguments and blame. Jealousy tends to cause a lot of drama within your relationships and causing a lot of toxic energy to manifest itself.

- You fear being rejected by your partner, especially when they seem to be achieving more than you do.

- You feel the need to have the last word all the time, in every argument especially. It is always about you and your opinions, and you don't spend enough time thinking about how your partner feels or what they have to say.

2: How to Build Healthy Habits as A Couple

How many times have you looked on with envy at other happy couples whom you know? Or even the happy couples that you randomly see around you gazing lovingly into each other's eyes or holding hands as they stroll through the park? They seem almost picture perfect, don't they? But of course, every relationship comes with its own challenges. These happy couples have just found a way to work through those challenges together by communicating well and relying on each other for support. That's the secret to their success.

Healthy Habits That Happy Couples Engage In

There are healthy habits which happy couples regularly engage in, and here are some practices you can begin applying in your own relationship to improve how you communicate with your partner or spouse:

- **Always Express Your Appreciation -** Do it all day, every day because you can never express appreciation enough. It is always better that your partner feels the extra love and appreciation that you feel for them instead of feeling underappreciated. Love the little things that they do? Let them know! You don't have to do anything elaborate, just simple little gestures, thank you notes, even text messages sent throughout the day letting them know how much you appreciate them can make a huge difference in someone's day.

• **Ask, And You Shall Receive -** Another healthy habit that a lot of couples tend to ignore is to just ask for what they want. Don't assume your partner is going to pick up on the little hints or read your mind and know how to anticipate your thoughts. Assumption is where a lot of communication breakdown tends to happen, which then escalates into fights that could have been avoided. If you want your partner to do something, don't be afraid to just **ask** for it.

3: Developing Emotional Intelligence

EQ is a concept which was made popular by Daniel Goleman in his book of the same title, **Emotional Intelligence.** In his book, Goleman outlines just how EQ is growing in popularity as people all over the world are beginning to grasp just how important this quality is in contributing to their success. It doesn't matter if that success is in their career or their everyday life, because either way, EQ is going to provide everyone with the foundation that they need to start forging better, more meaningful connections and relationships. It is forging those deeper, more meaningful relationships that is going to be the exact reason why developing your EQ is going to be important for improving communication skills within your relationship.

Signs That You or Your Partner May Be Lacking Emotional Intelligence

There are several signs which might indicate that you (or your partner) may need to work on improving your EQ. The signs that you want to look out for are:

• **Poor Ability to Control Your Emotions** If you find yourself losing your temper far too often, getting emotionally carried away in situations that have no real cause for it, you need to work on improving your EQ. Especially if you're guilty of the former, because anger can be an extremely disruptive force in any relationship which will cause it to eventually break down and deteriorate over time.

- **You Can't Read Emotions Properly -** A lack of self-awareness about the way others feel is also a sign of poor EQ. When you're unable to assess how the people around you feel, it becomes much harder for you to forge meaningful connections. Not only will you find it hard to relate to others, they too will find it hard to relate to you.

4: Developing Empathy Listening

Well done on making it to skill #4! Hopefully, you've been practicing everything that was learned so far up to this point. Once you have successfully improved your EQ levels, you are now ready to dive a little deeper into the **empathy** portion of it by developing your empathic listening skills.

Practical steps

- **You Need to Understand Yourself First -** Before you can begin to understand another, you must first work on developing a deeper understanding of **yourself**. Knowing who you are, why you react the way that you do is the key to begin developing a greater level of self-awareness. Take a step back and assess how you've been reacting to the different situations in your life and relationship this far and ask yourself, **why did I react that way?** Understand your emotional triggers, reflect on your actions, assess your emotions in detail, and do this as often as needed until you finally understand what makes you tick.

• **Naming Your Feelings -** Another great exercise which is going to enhance your self-awareness abilities is to name your feelings. Instead of just generalizing by saying **I am feeling happy,** define that emotion in greater detail. What level of happiness are you feeling? Cheerful? Joyful? Jubilant? Ecstatic? Practice this method, especially during the moments when you're experiencing those emotions intensely. Make a note of what triggered that reaction within you and then take a step back, assess the way you reacted at that moment and think about how you might have reacted better in such a situation.

5: Don't Be Afraid to Show Weakness

In a loving, healthy and happy relationship, you shouldn't have to hide who you are. You should feel so comfortable that you don't feel the need to pretend to be someone that you are not. That special connection between two people is what makes life meaningful. In fact, it is hardwired within our brains to **want** to have these connections with the people who are in our lives. Families, communities, friendships, work, romantic relationships, these connections are all forged because there is something within us that wants to feel that closeness to another human being.

Developing your empathy listening skills is much easier than you think too.

- **It's About Them, Not You -** The first thing that you need to work on to start developing your empathy listening skills is to remember that it's **not about you, it's about them.** It is always about them when someone is trying to have a meaningful conversation with you. This is the time for you to put your needs above others. It can be a challenge to put your personal feelings and opinions aside for a few minutes but remind yourself that this is someone you love that's coming to talk to you. If you love them, then it's time to make it all about them for the next few minutes.

• **No Distractions -** The minute your partner comes to you and says they want to have a conversation, put away all distractions so you can focus on them for the next few minutes. Put your phone away, put your computer away, turn off the TV, anything that's going to pose a distraction, put it away. For the next few minutes, your only point of focus is going to be your partner and listening to what they need.

• **Listening Actively -** There's a very big difference between listening, and listening **actively**. You could be listening and nodding along, saying all the right things, but your mind is actually a million miles away or thinking about something else. That's not active listening. Active listening is when you take in everything that your partner is saving, process it and stay engaged throughout the entire conversation. You know exactly what to say, when to say it and how to say it because you have been paying attention. That is active listening.

6: Understanding Body Language

Did you know that 55% of our communication is demonstrated through our body language? This was certainly a very interesting revelation by the author of Silent Messages, Dr. Albert Mehrabian. According to Dr. Mehrabian, only 7% of our communication occurs through the use of words, and that, compared to body language, is a very small percentage. It, therefore, goes without saying that body language plays a very important, if not crucial role, in being able to effectively communicate in relationships.

How Does Your Partner Behave During an Argument?

When you notice the following signs which signal disapproval, feelings of aggression or anger, it's time to take a step back and start to approach the argument differently:

- Nostrils flared

- Teeth bared
- Sneering
- Arms crossed tightly in an angry manner across the chest
- Frown between the eyes
- The body turned to point away from you
- Pointing or jabbing you
- Clenched fists
- Invading your personal space
- Posture is stiff and rigid
- Contracted pupils
- Rapid body movements
- Rubbing the back of the neck

IImage 6: Free Credits

7: Learning to Talk About It

Having difficult conversations can be, well, difficult. Unfortunately, as much as we would like to avoid having these discussions, it is not always possible. In any relationship, there is going to come a time where you're going to have these difficult conversations, especially in a romantic relationship where you're sharing so much of your life with another individual.

Why You Need to Learn to Talk About It

Because you can't avoid problems and issues forever. There is no "wishing it would go away" or sweeping it under the rug and pretending like it doesn't exist. That's not a healthy relationship, and it won't be a recipe for a long-lasting relationship either. No, whether you like it or not, you need to learn to talk about it.

The more you ignore your problems, the harder they will be to fix. In a scenario where your partner may want to talk about and address these issues but you don't, it can cause a lot of frustration, tension, and resentment over time. Your partner will get frustrated eventually over your refusal to talk things about, and eventually, it will cause your relationship to break down, possibly even end, if your partner feels like they are getting nowhere with you.

Relationships are not easy, and conflict is something that comes along with the package. While conflict and the issues that arise are sometimes beyond your control, what you **do have control** over is how you handle and manage the situation.

8: Digitally Disconnecting

Does your partner complain that you're on the phone far too much? Or perhaps it happens far too often where you want some quality time with your partner, only to find that they're not 100% present with you because they're too preoccupied with scrolling through social media?

Here's how you can start digitally disconnecting from your devices to improve your communication as a couple:

• **Set Expectations -** Understandably, disconnecting for an entire day or maybe two is not entirely possible for many couples. The key is to find a middle ground that works for both of you by setting expectations. Start by committing to setting aside one hour each day to spend time with each other without your phones, tablets or computers present. Both partners need to come to an agreement to commit to spending this quality time together, and as it becomes a habit, you can slowly move onto increasing the amount of time spent, provided you're both in agreement with it.

• **Set Tech-Free Zones -** Set up some zones around the home which are "tech-free". The bedroom for example, or the family room, maybe even the dining room during meal times could be set up as spaces where you're not going to use technology during the times that you're there. This allows you to focus instead of having conversations with your partner instead of constantly checking for the next email or social media update. This could be great for improving your sleep patterns too.

9: Apologizing Mindfully

When you apologize to your partner, how often do you **mean** it? Apologizing and saying all the right words is easy, but apologizing **mindfully** requires that you think about what you're saying and say it with emotion and feeling. Mindful apologies are more meaningful because of the sincerity and genuine feeling that is involved.

Anyone can just utter the words **I'm sorry** for the sake of doing so, or because it is expected of them. But is an apology for the sake of doing so **really** an apology at all?

Apologizing mindfully can open the door to much better communication and healing in the relationship, and here's is how you do it:

• **Don't Just Feel Remorse, Express It -** Put emotion and feeling behind your words when you apologize. With the emotional intelligence skills, you have developed, empathize and put yourself in your partner's shoes. How would you feel if you were in their situation? Being authentic and genuine with your apology requires you to feel the hurt that they could be feeling, and in doing so, feel remorse over having hurt them in that way.

• **Don't Wait to Apologize -** It is also equally important to apologize as soon as you realize that you were in the wrong. Don't wait until tomorrow, next week or next month to do it, because it then loses all meaning. The hurt and the damage has been done, and if you don't do something at that moment to fix it, it might end up being a case of too little too late.

10: No Judgment Zone

Judgment. It is among the most damaging forces that a relationship could experience, aside from anger. Whenever you judge someone, especially your partner, the message that you're sending them is that you don't accept them for who they are. In turn, the hurt emotions that they experience from your judgment will build up resentment within them and over time, the relationship will fall apart.

How to Stop Judging the People We Love

Now that we know that judgment is a damaging force in any relationship (not just the romantic ones), the next question that we need to ask ourselves is **how do we stop**? You can still save your relationship before it's too late, here's what you need to do to stop judging your partner:

- **Don't Expect Them to Be Like You** - Your partner is doing their best, and giving it their best in your relationship. They're doing the best that they know how, based on their experiences and what they've been through in life so far. Nobody would purposely be on their worst behavior. This is what you need to remind yourself of, and why each time you find yourself about to judge your partner, remember that **they are not like you**. The sooner you let go of that expectation, the quicker you'll be able to learn how to stop judging the one that you say you love.

- **Listen to What They're Saying -** When we often find ourselves judging our partners, we're not listening. You've already mentally blocked yourself off and all you care about at that moment is how **you feel** and what **you think.** This especially happens during an argument, when you disagree with what your partner is saying and you judge them for it. Again, you're going to have to rely on emotional intelligence to get you through this. Empathize, take a step back and try to **actively listen** to what they are telling you and see the truth in what they say. Understand that whatever it is they are telling you, it is how they perceive things from their point of view, and there's nothing wrong with that. Keep an open mind and you will learn how to judge less.

11: Working on Yourself First

This is going to be a very important chapter as you work on your self-improvement. If you want to become an improved version of yourself and improve your romantic relationships, then you don't just need to focus on improving the external aspects, you need to focus on what's within, too. The very reason you picked up this book is that you want to improve the communication that happens between you and your partner to become the better version of yourself for the sake and health of your relationship.

Self-Improvement Begins with You

The choice to improve yourself starts right now, at this very moment. You have the choice to improve your life today and here is how you begin reshaping your mindset for the better:

• **Learning to Be More Flexible -** Learning to be flexible is an important step towards building a healthier, more positive way of thinking because if you don't, you will find it difficult and frustrating to overcome bumps in the road when things may not be going your way. You can't control everything, especially when it comes to relationships, and learning to be flexible is how you cope with the ups and downs and challenges that come your way. Being flexible is how you learn to work better together with your partner as a team, the way that it should be.

• **Stop Focusing On Your Failures -** The mistakes of the past have a way of haunting us if we don't find a way to deal with them and let them go. This baggage that we carry with us and bring into the new relationships that we forge are not healthy for either party. Reshaping your mind includes changing the way you see failures because as you work towards improving yourself, you are going to have to overcome a few challenges which may sometimes take a few setbacks and tries before you get it right. Instead of viewing failures as "failures", see them as learning lessons instead and use them as a gauge of what works and what doesn't.

12: Using Irony to Diffuse Unpleasant Situations

Forging connections to today's modern world isn't as simple as one might expect. We are surrounded by all sorts of technological devices and gadgets which are supposed to bring us closer to the ones we love and the people who matter, yet somehow we seem to be more **disconnected** than ever, and we struggle to form intimate human connections sometimes. Talk about irony, right?

Should We Use Irony in Our Relationships?

Relationships are a complicated system. If your partner has a sense of humor, yes it can certainly be used to help diffuse unpleasant situations, because it helps the two of you to see the funny side of things. Perhaps even get a couple of good laughs or two. But as for whether irony is the **best** approach to take? Well, perhaps not all the time. It can be either a good thing or a bad thing, depending on how you perceive it and how you use it within your relationship.

The thing about relationships is that it involves two people coming together, trying to work together to create harmony. When there's a disagreement over the way things are done, middle ground and compromise must be created so that both parties end up happy and satisfied with the outcome. When you know that in certain situations, using irony might upset your partner even more, so try to meet them halfway and figure out another approach to resolving the unpleasant situation.

Instead of irony, what might be better is to use humor to help relieve the tension that is sometimes felt from time to time. Being able to laugh what brings people closer together, and having a sense of humor has always been recognized as an important quality to have in a long-term relationship. Humor is merely about the funny things that get said, it is also about the things that you do together as a couple. It is about having **fun** in each other's presence, and indulging in activities that make you laugh.

13: A Couple That Laughs Together, Stays Together

If you could choose what the absolute favorite was, what would it be? Would it be that you laugh together a lot as a couple? Have you experienced that laughter which leaves you in stitches? Cracking up so hard that you can't help the tears from pouring down your cheeks and your sides aching so hard you feel as if you could never stand up again? That kind of laughter is a magical thing that can bring two people together in exceptional ways.

How Laughter Can Benefit Your Romantic Relationship

Among the benefits that you stand to derive from having a sense of humor in your relationship include:

- **It Makes You Feel Physically Much Better -** Have you ever noticed how good you feel after a good laugh? How your spirits have just lifted and suddenly things don't seem so bad? Laughter is one of the most healing experiences we can go through as a human being, and it can physically do wonders for you better than any modern day medicine can. It releases endorphins in your body, which is the body's natural feel-good chemical, lowers your blood pressure, puts you in a relaxed state and even helps to lower stress.

- **It Lowers Your Inhibitions -** It's hard to feel defensive, angry or on the edge when you're feeling good and laughing. Especially if you're doing it with your partner, which is why humor is a much better situation diffuser than irony ever will be.

- **It Helps to Improve Your Communication -** Want to improve your communication between you and your partner? Use humor and laughter to do it. When a situation is tense and you think it's not going well, sometimes, a well-timed appropriate joke can help to break the tension and bring a smile to your partner's face. When you learn to laugh together about some of the challenges that go on in your life, it can sometimes help to put things into perspective, and even provide you with a creative solution you might not otherwise have thought of in your otherwise tense situation.

Image 7: Free Credits

14: Don't Neglect the Sexual Aspect

The sexual aspect of a relationship can cause a lot of worry and anxiety for many. Thanks to social media and movies and the unrealistic expectations they have set for romantic relationships, the pressure to perform in the bedroom can be overwhelming. Without proper communication going on, a relationship can quickly break down in the bedroom thanks to stress, anxiety, worry, and the fear that you're not living up to your partner's expectations.

Anxiety Over Sexual Relationships

Couples who are dealing with sexual intimacy issues are often susceptible to experiencing anxiety and fear, along with a wide range of worries that accompany those emotions. Among the things that may be running through a person's head when they worry about their intimate relationships include:

- They worry about being judged by their partner

- They suffer from low self-esteem and constantly find themselves worried about everything

- They constantly need to be reassured, sometimes on a daily basis and no matter how much your partner does his or her best to reassure you, it never feels like it is enough.

- They are unable to enjoy the sexual aspect of their relationship because they are more worried about whether they doing it right and whether they're satisfying you enough.

- They find it difficult to believe that their partner is happy with the sexual aspect of the relationship, despite the reassurance.

- They may find it difficult to be intimate because they are so full of worry.

- They experience a decrease in their sex drive as a direct result of that stress and worry.

15: Getting Some Space

It is easy to lose yourself in a romantic relationship. Being caught up in the romance, trying to please your partner and keep them happy and wanting to spend as much time around them as possible can make you forget what life was like **before** you ventured into the relationship. You could easily get caught up in wanting to do all the things that your partner loves to do that you eventually neglect your own interests over time.

Why it becomes easy to lose ourselves in another person is because their happiness can take priority over ours - especially in the beginning. Because we love them, we want to do everything we can to make them happy and that becomes our number one priority. In doing so, we forget that there are other aspects of our lives that bring us meaning and happiness, even before we found our partners.

Why Getting Space Is Important

Especially when you live with your partner, it is important to find some time to do things independently and on your own. Neglecting the things that you like to do - hobbies, interests, passions, and activities - puts you in a dangerously unhealthy relationship. What's going to happen when your partner isn't around? You're going to find yourself completely at a loss, possibly even losing a sense of who you are, which has often happened with a lot of relationships where couples rely too heavily on each other.

The healthiest relationships are the ones where the couples are able to find a balance. They have common shared interests which allow them to bond and grow together as a couple, but they also have other interests which are independent of just themselves.

It is important in every relationship that you maintain a sense of independence because:

• **You Need to Maintain Your Individuality -** If you're always so consumed by just the things that your partner loves to do, you're losing a lot of what makes you unique. It is part of your identity and who you are as a person. Maintaining a relationship with yourself is just as important as maintaining a relationship with another person. If you don't get to know yourself, you will never be able to love yourself.

• **You Are Able to Contribute More to Your Relationship -** You may be part of a relationship, but you are also your own person, and the individual qualities that make you great are what you contribute to making your relationship even better. When you're comfortable and happy with who you are as a person, you'll realize that you have so much more to offer. You don't need another individual to make you whole because **you are already whole enough.** Having your significant other in your life is just adding another element which brings you more happiness because now you have someone to share your life with.

16: Setting Goals Together

A goal can set you down a very powerful path. As a couple, creating shared goals to work towards is one of the most powerful exercises you could do to improve not just your connection, but your communication. Working on shared goals together can be fun, especially because there is nothing better than doing things and sharing successful accomplishments with the person that you love.

Goals help to turn that everything you envision as a couple into a reality. Every couple wants to see their relationship going somewhere, and setting goals to work towards will help give you something to focus on.

How to Start Setting Goals as A Couple

Setting goals as a couple is about creating a vision that you share together and then making a commitment to achieve that vision. Setting goals as a couple is not at all complicated, and in fact, here are some simple but effective strategies to help you get started:

- **Defining the Areas of Importance -** There's a lot of things going on in a relationship, and while you may be tempted to tackle all these areas, try to take it one step at a time. Goal setting should start in the areas which matter the most to both of you as a couple. These areas could be for example marriage, family, finances, kids, or even buying your first home together. It can be anything that you want, as long as it is an area that you think is important to your relationship.

- **Talk About It and Write It Down -** Set some time to sit down and have a discussion about what goals you and your partner hope to get out of the relationship. Write down each goal that you have (ask your partner to do the same), and then compare the goals which you have written down and see if you've got anything in common. If there are different goals that you both would like to achieve, brainstorm what you can do to meet each other halfway, or help each other to realize these goals so both parties are happy and satisfied with the outcome.

17: Don't' Hold onto Anger

If there is one emotion that is present and exists in everyone, it is anger. It is considered one of our core emotions, like happiness. It happens even to the best people. While anger is a natural emotion, it becomes a problem when it happens more frequently than it should, especially in romantic relationships. It becomes an even **bigger problem** when one or both partners refuse to let go of that anger and move on from it.

How to Start Learning to Let Go

The best thing that you could do for your relationship is to learn to let go. Don't expect your partner to "accept" your anger because this is who you are and this is part of your personality. That is entirely the wrong approach to use, and the only thing you are doing is making excuses to justify your behavior without having to do anything to change it. For the sake of your relationship, you are going to have to put in the effort to make a difference if you want to **see** a difference.

- **You Don't Need to Always Be Right -** There's no need for you to always be right and for one very simple reason. It's not worth it. By continuing to indulge in this behavior, you're not helping yourself or your anger issues. You are, in fact, making things much worse. Let go of the desire and the need to always be right. It will get easier over time too, and you'll feel a sense of satisfaction because deep down, you know that it is the right thing to do.

- **No More Room for Excuses -** The more excuses you make, the harder it will be for you to let go of your anger. There will always be a reason for you to **not** let it go. A reason to be angry, a reason to feel annoyed. There will always be a reason as long as you want it to be. Let go of the excuses and you will learn to let go of your anger eventually.

18: Sincerity Matters

Image 8: Free Credits

Communication is a process which takes a lot of work. **A lot of work.** If you're ever in any doubt about that, just remember the last time you and your partner had a conversation that you walked away from feeling extremely let down, heartbroken at being misunderstood, perhaps even feeling angry.

How to Start Building a Relationship Based on Sincerity

If you think that a lack of sincerity could be a problem that your relationship is dealing with right now that's potentially hindering communication between you and your partner, it's time to do something about it. The situation can still be fixed when acted on quickly enough, and here's how you start building a relationship based on sincerity:

• **It's the Promises You Keep That Make a Difference -** Each time you're about to make a promise to your partner, think of this old saying: **Don't make promises that you can't keep.** Making promises to your partner feels good, to see the smile on their face, but each time you make a promise that you can't keep, the disappointment leaves a little scar within them that chips away at their trust in you. Broken promises hurt, a lot and each promise that gets broken will make it harder for your partner to trust you the next time you make another promise, even when you're sincere about it.

• **Back Your Words Up with Actions -** Words alone are not enough to convince your partner of your sincerity if there's no action to back it up. Another apt saying which sums it all up nicely is **actions speak louder than words**. If all you're doing is using words to make your partner feel better but nothing ever gets done, it's the same as making empty promises that you can't keep.

19: Productive Conflict Helps

Nobody likes arguing with their partner. If we all could avoid arguments at all, we would. Some couples argue more than others do, and while arguments generally have a negative element associated to it, but there is such a thing as productive conflict, where arguing may actually be a good thing for your relationship.

Why Productive Conflict Is Good for Your Relationship

Now, you may be wondering how arguments can turn out to be a good thing for your relationship. Here is why handling a conflict in a productive way can be more beneficial for your relationship than you think:

• **Productive Conflict Enables You to Communicate Your Needs -** Arguing provides you with an opportunity to communicate your needs to your partner about what's making you frustrated. Arguments only become unhealthy when you allow negative traits like maliciousness, spitefulness, bitterness, and cruelty get into the mix. What a lot of couples don't realize is that arguments could be handled completely differently and in a mature manner. Use this as an opportunity instead to communicate with your partner and explain to them about why you're feeling the way that you are.

• **Productive Conflict Prevents You From Lashing Out -** You may not like having arguments with your partner, but believe it or not, it is much better than keeping everything bottled up inside. The problem with keeping in all that anger and frustration is that it tends to explode in the most inappropriate moments at times.

To prevent this situation is exactly why productive conflicts must be addressed, to keep you or your partner from lashing out in anger later on which could end up being much worse.

20: Developing Diplomatic Dialogue Skills

The words that you use during your communication process can have a big impact on the outcome. It isn't just about the tone of voice, but the **words** that you say which is going to have the biggest impact of all on your partner. For example, during a disagreement, you may not be shouting at your partner, but if the words that you utter during those moments are dripping with contempt, harsh and just plain insulting, you those words end up hurting your partner more than if you were actively yelling at them.

<u>**Bringing These Diplomatic Communication Techniques into Your Relationship**</u>

These are all wonderful traits which you can start bringing into your communication style with your partner and see what an improvement it can make in the way that you talk to each other.

• **Be Mindful of Your Choice of Words -** It is **very important** to be careful about the words that you use. Just one wrong word is all it takes to make a conversation go south and evoke a negative outcome or response. Your choice of words is important because of people's perceptions. Political consultant Frank Luntz even made this aspect a subtitle in his book entitled **Words that Work**, in which he summed it up perfectly by stating that **it is not about what you say, it is about what people hear.** When you're engaged in a productive conflict discussion with your partner, for example, avoid using aggressive words like **you must, you have to, never, always** which foster an element of negativity. Instead, replace those words with more diplomatic language, such as **why don't you consider, I think it might be better, have you ever considered perhaps...** Do you see how just a change of words puts an entirely different spin on the same message? To keep a conversation diplomatic between you and your partner, think about the words you want to use, then re-think about how you could make those words better, then **think yet again** about whether these are the best choice of words to use to achieve the outcome that you want.

• **Be Respectful -** It cannot be stressed enough how important it is to constantly be respectful throughout a conversation if you want to keep the peace. Respect goes a long way, and when you make your partner feel respected like their opinions and ideas are valued, you will see just how different the interaction is going to become. A little bit of an emotional intelligence exercise, here again, is to use empathy and put yourself in their shoes. If they were speaking to you disrespectfully, would you be inclined to just sit there and continue to listen without feeling any kind of negative emotion towards them? Highly unlikely. In fact, that is the quickest way to turn an argument bad, by being disrespectful to your partner when you're having a conversation with them because what you're doing is showing them that you don't care about their feelings at all.

Chapter 6: The advantages of building a conscious relationship

IImage 9: Credits Kim Magnago Photo

Good communication can be very challenging and rarely comes naturally to most people. It's something that needs to be intentional and it takes practice. If a couple isn't committed to improving how they communicate, they will most likely deal with certain patterns of miscommunication. This chapter describes the most common problems, including using the silent treatment and always equating talking with communication. This chapter also gets into how poor communication can play into emotional abuse.

- Important skills for related couples

While we've already discussed a few of the basic skills necessary for effective communication, there are a few essential abilities that we must harness and develop to maintain a healthy relationship. So, we'll go a little deeper into them here and try to break them down.

Listening

Hearing and listening are two completely different things. When we only hear someone, we can miss emphasis, words, and even whole ideas. But when we actively pay attention to the speaker and listen very eagerly, we become more effective listeners. The following skills below can help you improve your listening skills:

Clear your mind and avoid mental wandering. Don't get distracted by trying to decide what you want to say next or even focusing on other things on your mind.

Never interrupt them. Always allow them to talk without interruption until they get to the point that they need to make.

Maintain good eye contact. If you aren't looking at them, then they are likely to think you aren't listening.

Avoid clenching your fists, rolling your eyes, or shaking your head. These reactions can lead us to focus on what was said, and not what is being said now. Body language can easily encourage or discourage the other person to speak.

Stay away from distractions. Don't pick at your fingernails, go digging through your purse, or start paying attention to the television. These items can distract the speaker and make it difficult for you to actively listen.

Acknowledge what they say. Show that you are interested in what they are saying and encourage them to continue speaking with acknowledging responses such as "of course," "I understand," "okay," and even "uh-huh." Sitting in complete silence can make them feel as if we are not truly hearing them.

When it's your turn to speak, paraphrase what they

just said. This helps confirm that you have been listening, and ensure that you understand correctly before addressing what was said. And just to make sure you are both on the same page, you may want to summarize the discussion at the end of the conversation.

Pay attention to their tone and body language. This can clue you in on how they are responding to what you say and even hint at what they are thinking and feeling.

Let them know that you value what they are saying by responding constructively, even if you disagree. Stay away from ridiculing, criticizing, dismissing, or diverting the conversation.

Understanding Body Language

If you are correctly able to read someone's body language, you've already got incredible leverage on your hands right now. It is this very skill that is going to help you deduce how a person truly feels without them having to ever say a word, especially if this person is your partner. By being able to read these signals, you'll be able to anticipate their needs much better and support them in ways they may not even realize that they want at the time. A lot of body language occurs on a subconscious level, without us even realizing it. Our words may say that we're fine, but our bodies are telling a completely different story altogether.

Reading Your Partner's Body Language Correctly

In a relationship, your partner may be displaying a wide array of body language signals that signify what's on their mind or how they may be feeling at that time. Communicating effectively with your partner in any situation is going to depend heavily on your ability to read the signals that they are giving off, and better understand their moods so you will be able to adjust and moderate your responses and reactions to better suit the situation.

Body language can be complex, but at the same time, extremely fascinating. It is like unlocking clues to a puzzle, where the more you understand, the greater your awareness will be. In this case, the puzzle is your partner and what you're trying to do is understand how they feel without them having to tell you. Body language can give you clues into the feelings that they may not want to reveal, and when used correctly, can rapidly change the way that you and your partner communicate.

You don't have to be an expert to start picking up on the little body language nuances that your partner may be exhibiting. In fact, some clues are just a matter of paying attention and noticing the little things. That alone is going to make all the difference in the world in the way that you communicate and anticipate their needs.

Facial Expressions

This is where most of the body language signals are going to emit from - the facial expressions. Anything from the eyes, the lips, mouth, or even the way that they tilt their head is going to mean something. If your partner lifts their eyebrows, for example, this could signal skepticism, surprise or discomfort. If their mouth and lips are pursed in a thin line, it could mean that they are unhappy, irritated or angry. The clenching of the jaw which might happen during an argument could signal to you that they are stressed or angry.

Eye Contact

Another big one you want to look out for is eye contact. If, during a conversation, you notice that your partner's eyes are unfocused or looking behind you, for example, it could mean that they are preoccupied, distracted, anxious or maybe just not that interested in the conversation. Eye contact is another way of detecting when someone may or may not be telling the truth. According to several body language experts, whenever a person is telling a lie, they tend to look towards the left. They also struggle to maintain consistent eye contact the way a person would do if they were being honest. If you're trying to suss out whether your partner may be lying to you or not, look for these indicators and see how well they manage to maintain eye contact.

The Arms and the Hands

The arms and hand gestures are a bit of a tricky one because they could hold several different meanings. Crossing arms in front of the chest, for example, doesn't necessarily mean that your partner is closed off to the conversation or shutting you out. They could be doing this out of habit, because it's a comfortable position, or maybe because they happen to feel cold. You'll need to observe the context in which this gesture is occurring. If your partner crosses their arms in front of their chest halfway during a disagreement, for example, it means they are being defensive. On the other hand, if you notice that your partner has their palms facing up and outwards during a conversation, this is a good sign because it means they are relaxed, honest and sincere. If your partner clenches their fists, it could be a signal that they're feeling angry or tense.

The Proximity

How close someone chooses to be next to you is a signal about how they feel about you. If your partner chooses to stand close to you in a relaxed, comfortable manner, they are happy and comfortable being around you and being in your presence. If they move away from you however, it means the opposite.

Fidgeting About

Any fidgeting while sitting is a sign that your partner may be feeling irritated, bored or anxious. This is applicable too if they fiddle with their hands, or even objects in their hands. If you're about to have a serious conversation with them and you notice all these signs beforehand, you might want to think about postponing the talk to another time when they are much calmer. Ask them what's wrong when you see these signs at work and encourage them to talk about it, especially if they are feeling particularly nervous or anxious.

- Important skills for married couples

Focus on the Issue.

One way to resolve problems or share sensitive matters is to stay focused with the current issue. This means you should avoid bringing up the past or other problems. Stay focused on the present issue by trying to understand the immediate thoughts and feelings of one another. Use the word "I" more rather than using "YOU" in your conversations. This is one way of expressing your feelings without hurting your partner.

Image 10: Free Credits

Listen to Your Partner

Another technique to develop good communication skills for couples is to listen quietly until your spouse feels like you understand what they meant to say. Avoid interrupting your partner when he or she is talking.

When you fail to listen carefully while someone is talking, your response will be viewed as aggressive and insensitive since you will be focusing on what to say next. Some may even start sharing a response or comment before the one talking is finished. Always talk less and listen more.

Make Every Attempt to Compromise for the Best Solution

Another way you can practice effective communication is by looking to compromise. If a solution allows for it, try to include ideas, and recommendations from both partners to address or resolve a problem. Do not try to win and cause an argument just to have it your way. Instead, look for solutions that will meet everyone's needs. When you find a good resolution, both of you will be happy.

Don't give up. Keep working until you discover a solution. That is called brainstorming. An effective way to solve any conflict is by demonstrating your willingness to find a lasting solution. You should have and manifest a constructive attitude when solving any conflict. Never give up on communication when solving any problem in your marriage.

Understanding a Critical Communication Need and Solutions

A key problem surfaced and was identified as their conversation shifted and took a downturn from talking about the stated issue to yelling at each other. In one sense the secondary issue (how they attacked each other) became the primary issue. Together we were able to stop the emotional hemorrhaging by stopping the verbal attacks and directing them to a few techniques that could help them manage their language, stay focused on the real issue and ensure each partner had an equal opportunity to share their thoughts and feelings.

A Common Problem and Need

Couples, more than ever need to learn simple communication techniques and skills for the family to address problems and resolve issues. Below there are some basic principles, techniques and tools that can help stop negative communication, inspire or create a positive environment where couples and children can safely share their thoughts and feelings and help resolve real issues. If faithfully implemented, they can strengthen relationships at home and in the workplace.

Touch Each Other

One of the best ways to disarm a negative attitude during your sharing time is by gently touching each other when you talk. During your conversations it is good to sit close to each other and exchange a few touches by holding hands or even tapping one another. Even the smallest touch can make you feel more connected than ever. I believe an occasional smile may be as effective as a touch. Commit yourselves to creating a safe environment to share and communicate more often.

Demonstrating Respect for Your Partner is Always a Great Way for Improving Marital Relationships

When a couple commits to listen and mutually understand each through regular communication, they will have one of the most effective opportunities to demonstrate a deep respect for the relationship and for each other.

Use Kind Words in Your Conversations

Couples who use words such as thank you or I am sorry have few conflicts in their relationships. Use the "I" word and not "you" (you always, you never). This will place emphasis on your feelings and ideas instead of what you are upset about that your spouse is or is not doing.

Avoid Solving Difficult Conflicts After 8pm

After a full day of work and activities, you and your spouse are likely physically and emotionally exhausted.

Don't Force a Meeting

Respect each other's current physical and emotional conditions. The odds are it will not be successful as you won't have enough time to effectively talk through the conflict and you could end up going to sleep facing opposite walls. If necessary, request a "time out" and reschedule a specific appointment within the week so your partner knows that the issue will be addressed soon.

Seek Professional Help

The process of working out any problem in a relationship needs hard work from both partners. However, when you are unable to work through any problem by yourself, it is better to seek professional help from a counselor.

Give Yourself Time to Calm Down

If they have done something that truly upsets or angers you, of course, you need to discuss it. But that doesn't mean it has to be done right away. Give yourself 48 hours and if you're still upset, then start the conversation with the knowledge that you have given yourself time to reflect on the issue. If it is no longer bothering you, then you may want to consider just dropping it altogether.

Pick the Right Time to Have the Conversation

Pick a time when you both can discuss the issue calmly without distractions, stress, or being in a rush. You may even want to schedule a time to overcome any possible hurdles.

Always Keep Their Feelings in Mind

If you are in a relationship, then it stands to reason that you care about your partner and their feelings. Don't say something that invalidates their feelings for what they are saying.

Better communication is a skill that almost every relationship could handle some enhancement. Even when the subject matter is not important, or maybe even mundane, we should always attempt to fully communicate within our relationship.

Be Open

This may mean talking about things you have never discussed with anyone else but means you are being unabashedly honest and vulnerable with them. While this may open yourself up to possible disappointment or being hurt, it can also lead to opening yourself up to your partner and the full potential of all a relationship can be.

- Important skills for couples with children

Image 11: Free Credits

To start you on your journey in critical communications we are going to talk about kids. For most of us kids aren't really looked upon as people who we have deep and meaningful conversations with. In fact, most people will look at children as needing to be educated and told what to do rather than sit down with them and have a meaningful conversation.

Yes, it is true that there are topics and subject depending on the age rage of the child you may not be able to talk to them about or if you did they may not have the mental or emotional maturity to understand and react to the conversation but as a whole child are pretty smart, are extremely creative and uninfluenced by the adult baggage we carry with us.

What is their age?

When adjusting your mindset, you need to look at the age of the child. In today's day and age, it seems that children are growing up and turning into adults at five and six years of age but the truth is that they are still children and they need to be addressed as children.

Understanding of the world

What is their understanding of the world? With the introduction of the Internet and its wide spread acceptance and use in our day to day lives it is getting to be harder and harder to shield our children from these things as we once did. In today's world our children can find out pretty much anything that they want to know with a simple Google search.

As such it is critical that we understand their understanding of the world. With so much misinformation and conflicting information it is easy for them to become confused and form their own opinion on the world. When communication with children it is very important that you listen to them, watch what they do and educate yourself on their world so that it is much easier for you to communicate with them in theirs.

Educate yourself and them

In the education process of communication with children you as the parent need to educate yourself to their world. One of the most important aspect of this education will be their language. Throughout time starting back in the 1960's or so children began to come up with phrases, terms and their own universal language that makes perfect sense to them but is a foreign tongue to the rest of us.

When we were growing up the word "Cool" meant one thing and ten years later the word "Bad" means just the opposite. It is the constant shifting of these words, meanings and global understanding that makes communication so difficult.

You can begin to understand the context to their conversations and begin to pull our red flags that as a parent you will want to be aware of. From there you will want to start observing and monitoring their body language and communications. Now, I am not saying to go out there and spy on your kids or install Nanny Software on your kids computers but I am saying if you want to learn how to communicate with your kids or children in general it is important that you educate yourself with the same material that they are educating themselves with.

Lead by example

When it comes to communication with children words might not be the best way to get your point and meaning across. Again, depending on the age and emotional maturity of those you are talking to these actions may not fit but if you use actions over words then you may have a better communication medium to turn to.

When dealing with children not all children will do what you want them to do. In fact, the odds are they will probably do the opposite. So, what are you to do in order to get them to change their mindset to reflect yours?

The first thought would be to sit them down and talk to them like an adult. Again, they are not adults and trying to move them up into your position as an adult and expect them to understand is harder and less effective than other options. The next thought or option that many will turn to is punishment. To start with people will send their kids to their rooms, take away privileges. On the surface this seems like a good way to gain control and teach someone a lesson when in fact it just shuts down the lines of communication which in turn pushes people away from each other.

The final action that people will use for communication is physical and emotional abuse or intimidation. This is a tactic that should never be used and in fact destroys all lines of communication since those being abused will just shut down and do whatever it takes to keep things away from their abuser out of fear.

Be Patient

When it comes to communicating with children it is important that you be patient. You need to understand and adjust your mindset, education and actions according to each specific situation. Remembering and understanding this will go a long way to keeping the line of communication open.

Keeping the lines of communication open

And finally the best way to communicate with a child and anyone for that matter is to create a secure and welcoming environment. If we let children know that we are always there to talk, have proven that they can talk to us on a wide range of subject and that they won't get physically or emotionally abused then communication becomes that much easier.

Chapter 7: How to deal with serious problems

Image 12: Free Credits

When you are in a relationship with someone, showing them respect is of utmost importance. As a part of human nature, we have a tendency to grow lazy in how we show respect and appreciation for people the longer we know them. It is not uncommon to see two people in a relationship taking each other for granted and not entirely respecting each other. Most frequently, these individuals do not realize that they are taking advantage of each other and have no idea that it is hurting the other person in the relationship. As a result, it can lead to confusion, arguments, hurt feelings, and disconnect.

- Some useful exercises and examples

There are several therapy exercises for couples that center on practicing skills to help make you and your partner better listeners and reduce conflict while creating a more efficient and effective way for you to share how you feel. Utilizing these tools can help you to better express yourself and lead to a healthier and fulfilling relationship. Learning to turn communication into a strength as opposed to a liability will help ensure a much happier relationship and help you and your partner grow even closer as you gain a new level of appreciation and understanding of one another.

Active listening requires that you fully concentrate, respond, understand, and retain what has been said. Active listening is designed to help make it easier to discuss sensitive issues and to deepen your appreciation, empathy, and understanding of your partner.

Reflective listening is where you paraphrase what they have said back to them to confirm that both of you completely understand.

One of the single most effective ways to create a better and more efficient communication style is by only using positive language. Make a strong and concerted effort to adopt an encouraging tone along with non-abusive and non-accusatory words and phrases. Stay away from name-calling, swearing, and the ever unpopular "you always" and "you never."

Another great exercise is known as 'the miracle question.' This can help you to learn about your partner's desires and dreams as well as explore your own and gain an understanding what you both need to be happy in the relationship. Simply ask your spouse 'while you are asleep tonight, a miracle occurs. When you wake up in the morning, what changes would tell you that our life had suddenly gotten better?' While their answer may be a complete impossibility, it can still give you a lot of insight and be very useful.

Soul gazing is an intense exercise that can help couples connect on a much deeper level. The exercise is simple but can have a huge impact on the couple's sense of connectedness. Simply face your partner in a seated position and move close to one another so that your knees are almost touching. Look into each other's eyes and hold eye contact for 3 to 5 minutes while refraining from talking. If the silence is uncomfortable to you, put on some music that you both like and hold eye contact until the song is through. This exercise may be uncomfortable or awkward at first, but if you practice it a few times a week it will help deepen the connection between the partners and help strengthen the lines of communication.

A simple yet powerful exercise is called Uninterrupted Listening. This exercise is exactly what it sounds like. You simply set a timer for 3 to 5 minutes and let your partner speak. They can talk about whatever they wish and your job is to do one thing and one thing only: listen. You are not to speak until the timer goes off, completely getting your partner your undivided attention. While you may not speak while the timer is going, you are allowed to use your nonverbal communication skills to encourage your partner or to show empathy. Once the timer is up, switch places, reset the timer and complete the exercise again with you having the floor. This exercise can help the two of you strengthen the lines of communication by getting you to talk to each other just about your day or what is on your mind. This is a great exercise to use on a regular basis and you'll find that the more you use it, the more comfortable you both are sharing your day with each other.

Another easy exercise is called '5 Things,' and can be utilized anytime the two of you are together. You only need your imagination. You just come up with the theme, such as; "what I appreciate in you," "what I'm grateful for," or "what I would like us to do together." And then you each take a turn listing off five things within the chosen theme. Once you've finished sharing both of your lists, take the time to ask follow-up questions, comment on each other's answers, or come up with five more things together. This can be a very fun and engaging exercise that can help couples to connect and learn something new about their partner.

Mix it up a little. When we follow the same routine day in and day out it can cause the relationship to grow stale or even stagnant. Leave the distractions at home and share some time together in a new environment so that you can both relax and unwind. Taking a trip together it is a great opportunity for you to work on building those good communication skills while having a little fun together in a whole new place and creating new memories. This can also help alleviate any stress that could possibly be making communication more difficult for you. There are also some great couple's retreats where the sole purpose is to help you improve your relationship.

Learn to grow with your partner, not against or away from them. Of course, we all tend to grow, change, and expand our horizons over time but when you are in a long-term relationship can sometimes make it easy for us to be blinded to changes in our partner's likes, dislikes, interests, or even new aspects of their personality. Keeping the lines of communication open and attempting to share their interests or hobbies can help you stay in tune with any changes.

One last exercise that I want to share with you is a great little communication activity that is great for those needing to make changes or to solve difficult relationship issues. This exercise keeps the discussion light but can remind you of the special connection you have with your partner and help you learn more about them and yourself. As always, be mindful of your nonverbal communication and simply take turns asking each other a question from the topics listed below. You can make up your own questions for each category and don't be afraid to mix it up.

- Hopes and Dreams - such as, "what is the happiest life you can imagine?"

- The Fun Things - "what upcoming movie release are you most looking forward to?"

- About Us - such as, "was there a specific moment when you realized you are in love with me?"
- Work Life - "what is the most challenging aspect of your job?"
- Emotions - such as, "when were you the most afraid?" Or "what was the best day of your life so far?"
- Other Relationships - "who are you closest to in your family?"

By building our relationship skills and communicating effectively while utilizing exercises that enhance the connection between the couple, we can help ensure that we have a strong and long-lasting relationship. While there is no one set exercise that you can engage in to strengthen the relationship or to ward off separation or divorce, utilizing the exercises above can help you find your 'best practice' for your relationship.

Communication exercises + games

The last very useful way to improve your communication with your partner is to try out communication exercises and games. These are often employed in a couples therapy setting (which we'll talk about in the next chapter), but they're easy to do by yourself, too. You also don't need to be in therapy to get something out of them. Here are some good examples:

Twenty Questions

This classic game is really fun and can trigger some great conversations. Come up with 20 questions (or look online) for your partner and take turns asking and answering them back and forth. They can be really light-hearted like, "What's your favorite fruit?" or more serious, like, "When have you felt the most scared?" This is a great game to play during long car rides, at the end of the day, or whenever you set aside some time to focus on each other.

Look Into My Eyes

One of the more intimate games out there, "Look Into My Eyes" is all about vulnerability. Sit facing each other, close enough to hold hands. Look deeply into your partner's eyes for a few minutes, not speaking, and not looking away. Take note of the feelings that arise in you. After a few minutes, start talking about something, like how your day was. Stay in eye contact. When you've finished talking, it's your partner's turn. Go back and forth a few times. Afterwards, describe how this exercise made you feel.

Giving Thanks

At the end of the day, set aside some time with your partner. Both think about three good things that your partner did for you, whether it was helping you with the dishes, sending you a funny text, or giving you a back rub. Be sure to say, "Thank you." This exercise helps both people take note of the positive things in the relationship and express gratitude.

Highs and Lows

This game is a great one for daily check-ins. It's best played during the evening, but not too late, when both or one of you is really tired. Ask your partner what the high and low of their day was, and then share your own. While your partner is talking, practice good listening techniques like eye contact, nodding, asking questions, and so on. This will build empathy and encourage your partner to be open and honest.

Simon Says/Copycat

If you and your partner want to work on learning how to communicate clearly, this game (which isn't the traditional Simon Says) is fun and effective. First, one of you should draw something on a piece of paper. Think structures like boats, animals, and so on. Something that can be identified at first glance. Now, without showing your partner your drawing, walk them through how to copy it on their piece of paper. Don't tell them what is it, go line by line. Pretend as if they've never seen a cat or a boat, so those words don't mean anything. This game challenges your ability to communicate clearly in a way your partner understands, and it challenges their ability to listen.

- **Pointers and in-depth information in an informative and friendly way,**

As you continue building a stronger sense of communication with your partner, you also need to practice respecting them. Communicating effectively with your partner **is** a sign of respect in and of itself, but there are many ways that you can intentionally incorporate respect into your relationship so that your partner truly knows that you respect them. In this chapter, I am going to show you how you can use communication styles and techniques to show your partner a higher sense of respect.

Notice Your Partner's Needs, Desires, and Concerns and Act on Them

When you communicate with your partner, chances are they will regularly tell you what they desire, what they need, or what they are concerned about. Instead of simply hearing what they are saying and moving on, take it in and make a mental note of it. When you take a mental note and then later act upon what your partner has said, it shows that you care enough to take the initiative and support them in having their needs or desires fulfilled, or in feeling safe against whatever may be concerning them. This makes your partner feel special because you are going out of your way to put an effort into making sure that they are comfortable and happy.

You do not have to be at your partner's beck and call, but acting on what you hear in one way or another proves that you are listening and that you care about what makes your partner happy. This type of consideration and effort makes your partner feel as though you genuinely care about them and their happiness or well-being, and increases the sense of closeness that they feel toward you.

Do Not Procrastinate When Your Partner Asks for Something

If your partner asks you for something, make sure that you do not take your time and procrastinate in getting it done. Procrastinating shows that you do not care about what your partner has asked and can make them feel unimportant or unworthy of having your help. This can show your partner that you are not concerned about helping them or supporting them in getting things done which can lead to your partner feeling frustrated, unimportant, and even neglected if it happens often enough.

Doing things in a timely matter after your spouse asks for something to be done shows that you care enough to make it a priority. This directly translates to you considering them to be a priority in your life, which makes them feel important and cared for. While you do not have to immediately jump up and start doing something the moment your spouse asks, getting to it as soon as you reasonably can is important and says a lot to your partner. Remember, your actions speak louder than your words. This type of action proves that you care for your partner and that their needs matter to you.

Be Kind and Gentle with Your Sense of Humor

When you are in a relationship with someone, you know them more intimately than virtually anyone else does. This means that you know what can upset them, hurt their feelings, or lead to them feeling uncomfortable or even unsafe. A great way to show respect to your partner is to be considerate about these factors when you are joking with them. Do not make a joke about something that you know could upset your partner or that may trigger unwanted feelings in them. Instead, be more considerate and avoid jokes on topics that could be hurtful toward your partner.

On that note, if you hear your partner talking in a more serious tone or attempting to address a more serious topic, be considerate toward their needs. Realize that this is them needing to have a serious conversation and do not begin bringing humor into it or talking away from the conversation by not taking it seriously. Take your partner seriously, take their topic seriously, and address it accordingly. Nothing is more challenging than approaching a difficult conversation and feeling like you are not being taken seriously or met with compassion. Show your partner respect by helping them to feel understood and safe when discussing serious topics with you, even if you do not fully understand why it is so serious to your partner.

Do Not Hold Your Partner Hostage for the Past

When you are in a relationship for a long time, it can be easy for the old pain to be brought up by new experiences. For example, something your partner did in the past that hurt you could be re-triggered by something new that they did that was similar in nature. When this happens, you might feel compelled to dredge up the past and use it as evidence to prove that they had an evil plan to try and hurt you, or they do not consider you and your feelings. While it is important to address ongoing trends that you feel reflect you being mistreated, it is also important that you decide if it really constitutes as a trend or not. If they do it constantly, then it is likely a behavior that needs to be addressed. However, if it has only happened a couple of times in your relationship or the two are not actually as closely linked as you initially believed, chances are it is not actually a trend. Instead, it is likely just a mistake that was repeated because your partner did not know any better or did not realize that you would be hurt by it. Chances are, if the last time happened a long time ago, they may not have realized that it would come across as them repeating a seemingly negative or hurtful behavior. As such, this instance should be seen as isolated from anything that happened in the past.

Letting your partner know that the past is forgiven and put behind the both of you proves that you are not going to continue holding them hostage for everything that they have done. Chances are, your partner wants to move on from the past just as much as you do. If you continue to hold it against them, though, you prevent either of you from moving on and you hold your relationship in a permanent state of hurt. Let go, forgive, and treat each experience as a new one unless it is a behavior that happens frequently. In that case, bring it up as a behavior to be addressed on its own, rather than using it as a weapon during an argument to try and prove that your partner is somehow "bad" or "evil" and intentionally hurting you.

Avoid Using Sarcasm in Conversations

Sarcasm can be a fun tool used to amplify a joke or to play with as humor. However, when it is used during standard conversations or in arguments, sarcasm can be hurtful and demeaning. It is important that unless it is very obvious that you are using it in a joking manner and that it is an appropriate time for jokes, that you avoid using sarcasm at all.

You should avoid showing contempt for what your partner is saying. Rolling your eyes, gawking at what they are saying, or otherwise acting like what they are saying is wrong or worthless is unkind. In doing the show, you show a complete disregard for your partner and disrespect toward their thoughts and opinions. This can be hurtful and demeaning. Instead, focus on showing your partner that you are compassionate toward them, even if you do not understand where they are coming from at the moment.

Show Compassion, Empathy, and Consideration

Showing a sense of compassion, empathy, and consideration toward your spouse is essential. This is one of the strongest ways that you can prove to your spouse that you care about them and that you have respect for them. Compassion, empathy, and consideration all work toward showing your partner that you understand where they are coming from and that you have respect for their perspective. When you use compassion, empathy, and consideration through your communication styles, you help your partner feel safe in expressing themselves around you. As a result, they feel as though it is safer for them to be vulnerable around you, and they are more likely to open up. Through this vulnerable sharing, your relationship will grow a deeper emotional connection which results in greater intimacy and more closeness between both of you.

Acknowledge Your Partner and Pay Attention to Them

Your partner not only deserves to be acknowledged and to have your attention, but they also long for it. A relationship where one or both partners is rarely acknowledged or given enough attention from the other partner is one that will never last. In romantic relationships, people crave closeness, attention, affection, and admiration.

Your partner wants you to acknowledge them, acknowledge their achievements, and acknowledge the things that matter to them. They also want you to give them your undivided attention from time to time. When you do, you prove that they are a priority to you and that you respect them enough to set aside any distractions and give them your undivided attention on a regular basis. This is a wonderful time to show your admiration and appreciation, too, helping you both feel even closer.

When you show your partner respect by acknowledging them and paying attention to them, you not only help them to feel more appreciated and loved, but you also bring you both together.

Chapter 8: improving dialogue, intimacy and eliminating anxious attachment

Image 13: Free Credits

If you take the time to open good lines of communication at the beginning of a relationship it can help you immensely as you move forward together. Of course, it goes without saying that honesty is extremely important at this time so no matter what, be honest with yourself and with your partner. In this chapter, I'm going to cover several key areas and ideas, as well as give you tips for getting some of those awkward conversations started.

Of course, sex is generally a big part of any relationship but it is usually even more so at the beginning. While these can be some of the most difficult conversations to have, especially with a new partner, there are certain ones that you will want to have even before you have sexual relations.

- Improves dialogue

What type of relationship are they looking for? Friendly or romantic? Sexual or non-sexual? Committed or non-committed? Monogamous or not? If you don't match up here you may want to reconsider going any further?

When was the last time they were tested for an STD/STI? Which ones were they tested for and what were the results? How many partners have they been with since their last test? Did they use protection? This is also a good time to ask if they have ever shared a needle with someone for tattoos, drugs, or piercings because unfortunately some STI's are transmitted this way.

What about birth control? Which methods do they prefer/use? Is there any possibility of a current pregnancy? Are they open to the possibility of pregnancy? Protecting yourselves from unintended STI's or pregnancies shows that you are responsible and that you care, setting some solid groundwork for open lines of communication. And just remember that the best time to discuss safe sex is before you move to the bedroom. A really good way to start the discussion is by telling them that you truly care about them and you want to ensure that you're both protecting each other and the relationship. You may want to start by voicing your own preferences first as this may make your partner feel more comfortable with the discussion. In this day and age, it is also not a bad idea to go get tested together for mutual support.

The same goes for safer-sex. Do they utilize dental dam or other barriers? What activities do they enjoy without the use of barriers? There are all important conversations to have on this subject and should be discussed as early in the relationship as possible. It is completely natural to feel a little embarrassed bringing the subject up but both you and your partner will be glad you did. Take the guesswork out discuss it early on.

Reflecting back to our previous chapter this is a perfect time to communicate your likes/dislikes when it comes to the bedroom. As you explore and get to know one another sexually, educate them on what kind of touch you enjoy or where and how you like to be kissed. You can and should also take this chance to set any boundaries that you are just not willing to try. Is there anywhere that you don't like being touched or kissed? Tell them now because remember, that shudder can be misinterpreted as joy and pleasure unless you articulate and let them know.

Are there activities or fantasies that you know you want to explore? Maybe there are some that you'd like to talk about or even role play or act out. Just remember to be receptive to listening to your partner's desires as well so again it is important to discuss boundaries before having this discussion to avoid making this conversation turn awkward. If you aren't comfortable discussing your fantasies you can try themed porn movies or books and share them together and when the time is right, start the conversation on it with something like, "I enjoyed the ___ scene. Maybe that's something we can try."

Something you both may find useful, and maybe even a little exciting, is making a yes/no/maybe chart. You both go off on your own and list out the things you know you enjoy (Yes), ones you don't like or are not willing to try (No), and then the one you might be interested in. Once complete then share your lists with each other and perhaps flip a coin to see who gets to have one of their Yeses used tonight. This can open some wonderful door for communication and also give you some revealing insight on one another.

Many people learn what they like and don't like by having sex with a partner while others utilize masturbation to get to know their bodies. When you learn how to give yourself orgasms it can make it easier to do so with a partner. Do you like it fast or slow? How much pressure feels good? What makes you uncomfortable? Once you know how to please yourself it is much easier to be able to show your partner how to touch you. You can also crank this up a notch by masturbating in front of each other so you can show them exactly how and then work it into mutual masturbation and take it slow, talk to each other and verbalize clearly when they do something right or wrong.

While talking about sex can be a little awkward or even scary, it can also be very eye-opening and even a turn-on. You can always start the conversation about sex by directly asking them what feels good or what kind of bedroom fun they are interested in. And then you can follow-up by letting them know what feels good to you or what you are wanting to try.

- **Improves intimacy**

Image 14: Free Credits

Intimacy is a natural and necessary part of marriage. Intimacy is what sets your spouse apart from your friends and family because you bring them into your life in a way that is reserved only for them. When you take advantage of intimacy and build it in your marriage, your marriage will thrive. You and your partner will both feel a deeper emotional connection to each other, your bond will grow, and you will become inseparable. Every strong marriage thrives with the inclusion of intimacy.

Building intimacy in a marriage is not only about having intercourse and being physically close, either. In fact, intimacy starts with an emotional closeness which is built through communication. From that, a stronger form of more vulnerable and meaningful physical intimacy can grow. Knowing how to nourish intimacy in your relationship in both an emotional and physical capacity will support you in having the best marriage possible.

There are many ways that intimacy can develop, each of which takes time and effort. One thing that you must realize is that intimacy grows from vulnerability, so you are going to have to get used to being open and vulnerable around your partner. Even though it may feel uncomfortable at times, peeling back your layers and taking down your walls to let them in is the only true way to develop emotional intimacy. That being said, you do not have to rush it and dash out too far beyond your comfort zone. Take it in steps and work on bringing them in at a pace that feels safe yet effective for both of you. The more you work on bringing your partner in and taking down your walls, the easier it will become. Plus, if you take your time and do it this way, it will be more sustainable as you will not suddenly feel overly exposed and have an emotional need to "protect" yourself once again.

If there have been any troubles in your marriage until now, emotional intimacy may feel particularly challenging. You might find that being intimate is hard because you feel as though you cannot trust your partner to accept you or understand you. Alternatively, you may have resentment toward them that makes you feel as though you do not want to let them get close to you. It is important to realize that if you do not overcome these barriers; your marriage will inevitably fail at some point. Instead, you want to work on overcoming these obstacles so that you can grow closer. If you need to, start by being vulnerable about how you feel and why it is hard for you to let your partner in. This can begin opening up the dialogue around feelings of safety and can support each of you in helping the other partner feel safer in your marriage. Then, as you both grow in feeling safer with each other you can begin moving into deeper stuff. Doing it this way is perfectly fine if this is what you need. Remember, be vulnerable in a way that brings your partner in but does not leave you feeling a sense of emotional distress. Take it slowly and build up to the closeness that you desire.

Discover Where Your Disconnect Lies

One excellent way to begin building intimacy in your relationship is to spend time identifying where it feels like disconnect exists in your marriage. When you take the time to identify what exactly or where your relationship is experiencing a disconnect, you create a foundation upon which both you and your spouse can work toward healing. This shows that you are both genuinely concerned about the disconnection, that you want to pay attention to what is causing trouble, and that you are invested in finding a solution.

Expressing where you are feeling the disconnection within your marriage can be vulnerable. Admitting to your spouse that you have been feeling underappreciated, emotionally neglected, taken for granted, unworthy, or unattractive can feel scary. On one hand, you do not want to feel as though you are complaining or calling them a bad lover. On the other hand, you want to make sure that your needs and desires are heard and that your partner understands where you are coming from. It can feel scary trying to voice your feelings and concerns, but it is also necessary. This helps you each understand where the other is coming from and look for solutions to support you both in sharing a stronger marriage.

If a vulnerability is something that has been lacking in your relationship, and in cases of poor communication it generally is, this is a great place to start. Opening up about your feelings and communicating even though it is a challenge allows you both to practice sharing those deeper thoughts with each other that you may have been hiding until now. It also allows the other partner to practice holding space, accepting, and appreciating that partner for being open and expressive. It is a great way to open up the two-way street of communication for stronger and more intimate marriage.

Apply Your New Communication Skills

Throughout this book, you have been learning plenty about trust, vulnerability, respect, compassion, and other valuable communication skills. In the process of building intimacy, these skills are going to help you in creating a stronger and more intimate marriage. Each of these communicational techniques is designed to help you connect more with your partner, creating a stronger emotional bond between the two of you. As a result, your intimacy will grow as well.

Putting an honest effort into incorporating each of these techniques into your marriage will help you to have a stronger marriage. This will work even better if you both work together on incorporating these communication styles. As you do, keep the communication open about how it feels and what emotions are coming up. You might find that you can support each other in having stronger communication styles and that by being honest about whether or not it feels like it is working for you will actually bring you closer. If you feel that a particular technique is being used wrong or could be used more effectively in a different way, you can open up a conversation around that topic and share it with your spouse.

In many cases, working together on things and opening up the lines of communication on what it is that you are working on is a wonderful way to make sure that you both stay on the same page. You also naturally bond through the very process of growing together, which can support your intimacy even further.

Communicate During Physical Closeness

When people lack intimacy in their relationships, generally their physical touching and closeness are negatively impacted. The harder it is to be emotionally intimate with your partner, the harder it may feel to engage in many types of physical touching, from hugging and kissing to full on intercourse. This can further damage the intimacy between you and your partner and leave each of you feeling unappreciated or unattractive.

A great way to overcome these feelings is to communicate them and then begin practicing communication while you are expressing physical intimacy. Do not be afraid to tell your partner what you want or need, or what you do not like. If you are in need of a hug on a particularly bad day, do not expect your partner to read your mind. This is especially true if you have not been physically close for quite some time. Chances are, they have no idea what your physical needs are anymore and they need to learn once again. Asking for a hug and letting your partner know why can help you both by ensuring that you get the physical connection that you need and it can help your partner understand why you need it. In the future, they may begin realizing these cues and practicing these physical connections intuitively. In the meantime, be open to giving direction and verbally asking for your needs to be met.

In addition, do not be afraid to admit when something does not feel good to you or when you need space. Hiding how you truly feel for fear of hurting your partner's feelings, embarrassing them, or for fear of the intimate moment coming to an end can result in you feeling resentful and uncomfortable around your spouse. You should work toward feeling confident about truthfully expressing yourself, and your needs and desires regarding any act of physical intimacy.

Discuss Your Future Together

Discussing a future that you desire to share with your spouse is a great way to express and experience intimacy with each other. When you spend time dreaming about what future you desire to share, this develops a strong bond between you and your partner. Not only does it affirm that you do genuinely want to share a future together, but it also gives each of you the opportunity to understand each other on a deeper basis. You get an opportunity to learn about each other's dreams, desires, wants, and "must haves." You also get to learn about what the other person does not want, does not like, or does not look forward to.

Generally, we do not spend time planning or dreaming of our future with just anyone. Instead, we reserve these discussions for people whom we are close with or who we feel may be interested in being a part of that future with us. So, sharing this time to let your partner in and know that they have a strong and significant role in your future plans proves that not only there is room for them, but that you also think about having them in your future often. This helps your partner feel special and close with you.

Find Common Interests That You Can Share

Finding common interests that the two of you can engage in together is a wonderful way to increase intimacy in your relationship. Chances are, you have had mutual interests since the beginning. After all, mutual interests tend to be what draws people together as it gives us something we can relate to with each other. However, over time we may forget about our mutual interests or simply not take as big of an interest in them.

Spending time recalling your mutual interests and then setting the intention to actually engage in them together on a more frequent basis is a wonderful way to increase intimacy in your relationship. When you commit to doing things together that you both find amusing, it is a wonderful way to spend quality time together with a common interest or goal in mind. While quality time spent together without distractions is important, too, it can become boring or routine if you do it without doing anything else in between. Spending time together doing something you both love brings out your passion for your shared interest which puts both of you in a great mood. That great mood is then shared and results in positive attention being shared between the two of you, further increasing your emotional bond and intimacy.

Learn New Things Together

In addition to doing something together that you both love, you should also commit to learning new things together. There is something about learning and growing together that draws two people close, even if that something is nothing significant. Taking a cooking class together, learning how to paint, learning how to drive go-karts, or otherwise learning something new together is a wonderful way to bond with each other. As you both learn, you can teach each other and support the other to do better so that each of you grows and learns together.

Learning new things together has all of the same wonderful benefits that doing mutual hobbies together does. It really gets your positive endorphins flowing so that each of you is in a great mood. Then, because you are sharing genuinely happy emotions together, your emotional bond for each other grows. This is a wonderful time to shed the stress of your daily lives and have pure fun together, which is something that many struggling marriages lack. Setting the intention to incorporate this back into your relationship is a wonderful way to overcome the daily stress and mundane routines and reignite the passion in your relationship once again.

Commit to Learning about Each Other's Interests

Another interest you should focus on learning is about your partner's interests. Although you may not share in all of their interests, taking the time to understand what they are interested in will allow you to show how much you care about your partner. Furthermore, it allows them to bring you fully into their world.

Learning about your partner's interests does not mean that you need to become passionate about everything they are interested in. Instead, it simply means that you know enough that you can share in conversation about that particular passion or attend events pertaining to that passion. Your spouse will appreciate being able to share these parts of their life with you, especially if you take the time to understand them and engage in them with your partner.

Likewise, let your partner come into your world. Teach them about your interests and passions and give them the opportunity to know more about what matters to you and why. Share conversations with them and let them feel like they are a part of these parts of your life.

If you and your partner have certain areas of your life that you like keeping to yourself because they offer you a chance to have some personal time, you can still share these with your partner. However, you do not need to share them as extensively. Instead of inviting them to tag along, simply teach them enough that you can share a conversation after the event or later on. This allows them to feel like they are a part of your life and like you care enough to confide with them and bring them in, even if you are keeping it separate when it comes to actually physically engaging in the interest. Likewise, if your partner has something they want to preserve just for themselves, respect this desire but spend some time learning how to share in conversations about it so that they can tell you about it later and you are able to engage back.

Go on More Unusual Dates Together

Many married couples go years without ever having a date together. That or their dates are based around the same activities each time, such as dinner and a movie. While traditional dates are always a wonderful experience, it can become a little mundane. After a while, it may feel predictable and begin to lack the intimacy and connection that it used to bring to the two of you.

Regardless of which describes you better, not dating at all or having the same dates every time, it is time to change it up. You need to start planning more unusual dates with your partner. This does not mean that you need to do something together that is literally strange or unusual. Instead, it means to get outside of your normal and do something different together. Rather than going on a dinner and movie date, go to an arcade or to an adventure park together. Or, maybe you can go out of town and spend the night at a luxurious hotel and roaming a new city.

Planning for new and unusual things to do together takes you and your partner out of your routine and shakes it up a bit. As a result, you are more present and focused on the date and you gain more from it. This will support both of you in feeling closer because nothing will be habitual or predictable. Instead, it will be new and out of the ordinary.

If you date regularly, plan to go on a new and unusual date at least once every other date night. If you do not date regularly, it is time to start! You can still plan to have a classic date that both of you love, but incorporate fun and unusual dates into the mix too. That way you have a comfortable pass time that you can fall back on, as well as something new and unexpected that can bring you both closer together.

Start a Tradition Together

Starting a new tradition together is a wonderful way to bring your marriage closer. Ideally, your new tradition should be done on a weekly basis. Of course, you can incorporate traditions into your monthly and yearly lives, too! Traditions are a fun way to do something that is just between you and your partner. It is sort of like an inside joke, except without the joke. Instead, it is something just between the two of you that you share together.

Your tradition can be as simple as going for a walk around the block every Saturday evening, or more elaborate like Sunday brunches. You can include weekly movie nights, a night where you both cook a new meal together, or a games night. Truly, you can choose anything that you desire.

Setting a weekly tradition that you can both do together gives you something to look forward to. These traditions are something that you share between the two of you and that gives you something fun to incorporate into your lives. In otherwise busy schedules that can draw you apart and keep you both preoccupied and on the go, these traditions are a wonderful time to unwind, unplug, and share some fun time together.

Spend Time Reminiscing on Your Shared Past

Long conversations about many different topics are a wonderful way to incorporate some intimate time together. This time can become particularly intimate if you begin sharing your favorite memories with each other. When you recall times in your past where you shared a great deal of fun, love, or passion, this helps you step back into those energies. You remember why you fell in love in the first place, why you love each other so much, and why you are married. As a result, it becomes easier for you to overcome any challenging feelings you may be having in the present because you remember the bigger picture.

Reminiscing with each other can be a romantic pass time too. Sitting together with your favorite bottle of wine or a hot drink and snuggling under the blankets while you laugh over shared memories can be a fun way to spend an otherwise boring or routine evening. Simply sharing this time together remembering your love for each other is a great way to grow that love even more and rekindle your passion for each other and thus, the intimacy that you share with each other.

Work Together on Household Things

Intimacy does not have to be reserved for scheduled moments and specific times. It can be enjoyed during your day-to-day lives, too. Sharing intimacy in your day-to-day lives can be as simple as doing household things together. Sharing responsibilities and doing them at the same time can be a fun way to bring yourselves together and remember everything that you share.

Looking over your finances, making dinner, doing the dishes, cleaning the house, and running errands are all activities that can be done together. This is also a great way to incorporate some quality time with each other while you are both busy with other daily tasks. As a result, you spend more time nurturing your relationship and feeling a stronger connection with each other. Intimacy does not have to be hard or scheduled. In fact, sometimes those candid moments of intimacy that are spent doing typical daily things can be some of the most meaningful moments of intimacy that you share together.

- Eliminates anxious attachment

Image 15: Free Credits

Conflict is an inevitable part of any relationship, especially when you spend a lot of time together and rely on each other for many things. Learning to deal with conflict effectively can ensure that anytime an argument arises in your marriage, you can overcome it by having the right tools on hand. If you are not effectively managing disagreements and conflicts, over time these smaller arguments can fester and turn into larger conflicts. As a result, it can drive a massive wedge between you and your partner.

Knowing how to handle conflicts and conflict resolution in a marriage is a tricky task as both of you will likely need to break many bad habits and learn how to communicate more effectively. It can take time and practice, so make sure that you are being patient with your partner and trusting in the process. The more considerate you are of each other, the easier it will be for you to begin integrating these new techniques into your conflicts and experiencing fewer arguments and resentment and more resolutions and forgiveness.

Avoid Turning Disagreements into Fights

One strong way to handle disagreements in your marriage is to avoid letting disagreements turn into fights. Disagreements generally occur before an actual fight officially starts, and learning how to recognize these disagreements can support you and your spouse in stopping them from turning into something bigger. Inputting your conflict resolution skills into the conversation when the disagreement starts, it can prevent it from spiraling. As a result, it will be less likely to turn into an actual argument and more likely to be resolved.

When you can avoid having arguments turn into fights, it is easier to handle resolutions. This is because the only thing that needs to be accomplished is finding a solution that both of you can agree on. If it turns into a fight, however, it might result in you also having to heal from hurt feelings and resentment.

Naturally, no one actually wants to fight with their partner; however, these fights can happen. Fortunately, there are two of you who are working together toward trying to end the conflict. This means that you can both work together to create a resolution that ensures that both parties are accounted for and respected.

Remember, a disagreement does not equal a fight. Part of avoiding having disagreements turning into actual fights is learning how to disagree without feeling personally attacked by the disagreement. This means that, while you can certainly feel frustrated and upset by the disagreement, you should not take it personally. Do not feel as though your partner is disagreeing with you just to hurt your feelings or make your life difficult. Instead, they simply have a different point of view than you do. Respecting that and understanding it can help you experience your emotions without becoming the victim and your partner becoming the attacker. As a result, it is easier to manage your emotions and prevent the conflict from turning into an actual fight.

Make Sure You Fight Fairly

In the event that a disagreement does escalate into a fight, it is important that you fight fairly. Fighting dirty can result in hurt feelings, pain, and resentment. As a result, it is much harder to come back from. If you do find yourself fighting, refrain from pointing blame, calling names, attacking someone based on their previous experiences, or using parts of someone's life against them. Trying to bully your partner so that they see that you are right or hurt them because you feel that they hurt you, is not okay. In doing so you can quickly destroy the trust and intimacy in your marriage and find yourselves feeling resentful toward each other and unwilling to come together to find a solution. This is not a healthy state to be in as it can result in no solution being found, or worse, it can result in your marriage ending.

When you are fighting, always make sure that you fight clean. Use compassion when fighting, do not get sarcastic, do not fight with contempt, and do not call your partner names. Doing so can result in you becoming a bully, and can be taken as a sign of abuse. Abuse at any point, even if it is unintentional during a heated fight, can be painful and difficult to heal. If it happens multiple times, it can result in major damages and a lot that both partners need to heal from.

If you have reached a point in your marriage where you feel that arguments are frequent and that one or both of you are bullying the other, it may be a good idea to incorporate a marriage counselor into the mix. Having someone who can mediate your conversations and help open up communication between you and your partner can help you both start the healing process and learn to communicate, and argue, in a healthier way.

Apologize When You Do Something Wrong

Never wait for your partner to ask for an apology. Instead, if you have done something wrong, admit fault and apologize for what you did. Not apologizing when you have done something wrong suggests that you do not care that you hurt your partner's feelings or that you are not taking responsibility for your actions. Both of these can result in your partner feeling like nothing will ever change and that you will both continue to have a poor relationship going forward. As a result, they may lose hope.

When you take the initiative and sincerely apologize for what you have done, it is easier for your partner to forgive you. This is because you are showing that you recognize that you have hurt them and that you feel bad for doing so. This also shows that you are willing to make the necessary changes so that you do not hurt them in the same way in the future.

If your partner claims you have done something and you do not recall doing it, you may struggle to apologize because you might feel like you do not want to take the blame for something you don't feel you have done. You should apologize anyway. Apologize for the fact that your partner feels as though you have hurt their feelings. Then, ask for them to elaborate on how you hurt their feelings and what you can do to avoid hurting their feelings again in the future. This shows that even though you might not understand right now, you are willing to try and that you want to make things right and treat them better in the future.

Take a Timeout If You Need To

During an argument, it is not unreasonable to ask for a timeout. When things get heated and feelings are being hurt or it feels like both your arguing is not productive, taking a timeout is a great way to relax, ground yourself, and remember what the goal is. Generally, the goal is for each partner to feel heard and understood and for a mutual agreement to be reached so that you can overcome the argument with a resolution.

If your argument has gotten to the point where no resolution is being considered or reached, where you feel like you are not making any progress, where feelings are being hurt, or where it feels like it is becoming too much, simply call timeout. Take some time away from each other and breathe so that you can let your emotions filter out and you can both come back into a clear thinking space. Then, you can approach the conversation again after you have both calmed down.

Make an agreement that upon calling for a timeout, you are both agreeing to calm down and come back to the discussion with the intention to find a resolution. You should also make sure that you both set a time upon which the conversation will be discussed once more. That way, both of you have clear expectations on when the other will be ready to talk again and no one feels as though they are being pressured to talk sooner than they are ready to, or like they are waiting indefinitely for the other partner to be ready.

Articulate the Real Reason You Are Frustrated

During a disagreement, it is important that you take the time to articulate the real reason as to why you are frustrated or upset. It is not enough to assume that your partner knows exactly what has caused your upset feelings. Instead, you need to take the time to explain why you are upset, what they did that contributed to it, and how you feel it can be resolved. This gives your partner a clear understanding as to what is actually being addressed in the conversation.

When you do not take the time to outline what it is that you are upset about, your partner is left guessing. As a result, they may assume that you are upset about something other than what has actually upset you. Then, they may be arguing in one direction about one topic while you argue in another direction about a different topic. This can lead to a great deal of miscommunication. Furthermore, it can lead to you both feeling as if you are not being understood. This can be frustrating because you feel as though you are explaining yourself well but your partner may think that you are referencing something different from what you actually are. As a result, it can lead to more hurt feelings and deeper argument.

Being clear on what has caused your frustrations ensures that your partner knows exactly what you are upset about. That way, they can address that exact topic rather than addressing something that is not related to your frustrations. This keeps you both focused on the same subject and working toward a solution.

Take Responsibility for Your Feelings and Opinions

During an argument, it is essential that you take responsibility for your feelings and opinions. Always use "I" statements to show that you are discussing your own thoughts and feelings rather than passing blame on your partner. Even if you are discussing something you said, discuss it in a way that shares that you are talking about your perspective of what they said and not what they actually meant. That way, if what you perceived and what they meant were two completely different things, it does not seem like you are feeding words into their mouth.

Furthermore, make sure that you are not considering your feelings and opinions to be absolute truths. Instead, they are **yours.** This means that you take the time to acknowledge that there are many different opinions, thoughts, feelings, and perceptions that can be considered true. When you take responsibility in this way and keep an open mind, you ensure that you are validating your partner, too. You do not want to get in an argument over who is right and who is wrong because chances are, both of you are right in your own ways. Knowing how to recognize this and respect it ensures that your discussion stays focused on the real issue and not a power struggle.

Make Sure You Break the Touch Barrier

During arguments, we have a tendency to create what psychologists call a "touch barrier" between ourselves and our partners. Essentially, this is a subconscious barrier that we put up as a way to protect ourselves from the perceived hurt that we believe our partner will inflict upon us. This actually ends up in us feeling a sense of disconnect from our partner, however, and can lead to a lack of trust and intimacy in our relationships.

When you get in an argument with your partner, or when anyone has hurt feelings for any reason, it is important that you break the touch barrier with your partner. You can do so by putting a hand on their shoulder, putting your hand on theirs, or hugging them to let them know that you still care even if you are disagreeing with them at the moment. Showing physical affection during arguments reminds your partner and you that you are still close and that you love each other. It also reminds you that your relationship is bigger than this conflict and that you can overcome it for the common good of your relationship.

If you do not break the touch barrier between yourself and your partner, this can lead to hurt feelings, resentment, and a lack of intimacy festering in your relationship. The longer it goes on, the more it creates a sense of disconnect in your relationship. As a result, you may both end up feeling emotionally and physically undesirable and neglected by your spouse. This can become a wound in and of itself which needs to then be healed.

When you are overcoming the touch barrier in your relationship, make sure that you are being mindful of your partner. Wait for an appropriate moment to approach them and hug them or break the touch barrier. If your partner has experienced abuse in the past, especially physical abuse, be extra gentle in approaching them. That way, you are respecting their space and their emotional triggers. Show compassion for their needs in the process as this will ensure that the breaking of the touch barrier improves intimacy, rather than results in them feeling fearful or hurt.

Stay Focused on the Bigger Picture

When you are in an argument with your spouse, always remember the bigger picture. Yes, you are in an argument, but no, you are not an argument. In other words, your relationship is far more than the disagreement that you are having. Remember that even though you may be feuding at the moment that there is still an entire marriage that exists between the two of you.

Gaining some perspective on your relationship and realizing that you are both in it for the same reason can support you in coming together on a solution. This is because you will realize that your argument is small in comparison to everything that you share together.

If you find that you are getting overly focused on the argument or that it feels like the argument is some sort of sentence for your marriage, stop and gain some perspective. Spend a few minutes remembering why you love your partner, why you are together, and what has brought you together. Once you remember why you are in a marriage with your partner, use this to support you in arguing with compassion and consideration toward them. That way, you both stay focused on finding a solution rather than arguing your case and being "right." It also prevents you from jumping to any rash decisions because of a moment of heated fighting.

Keep Your Argument Focused on the Real Cause

Anytime you find yourself arguing with your spouse it is important that you always keep your argument focused on the real reason why you are arguing. When your argument starts to get off topic, then this is when communication can become blurry and feelings can get hurt. At this point, you may begin dredging up past events and trying to use them to hurt your partner. Or, they may do the same back to you.

Arguments that get off topic can spiral quickly because they go from one isolated point of disagreement or hurt to a widespread point of disagreement or hurt. As a result, the amount of angry energy that comes into the mix can be challenging to come back from.

If you find that your argument is getting off topic, spend some time bringing it back into focus. Remember what you are upset about and bring it back to the main point. If you or your partner got off topic or began using other events to attempt to blame or bully the other person, stop and apologize. Then, make the mutual agreement to focus on what has caused this particular disagreement.

Often, when we find ourselves arguing about everything instead of the single reason that caused the argument in the first place, we never find a resolution. This is because we stopped looking for ways to resolve the conflict and we started looking for verbal weapons to hurt each other with. This will not be helpful for either of you.

Staying focused on the topic at hand and looking for a solution will be of great help. If you do feel that events of the past are unresolved, save them for a later date and come back to them with the specific intention of dealing with that particular topic. That way, each discussion is focused on a resolution and true solutions and healing can be found in your discussions, rather than more pain and frustration.

Show Respect for Your Partner's Perspective

Even if you do not agree, it is essential that you show respect for your partner and their perspective. When you stop respecting your partner's perspective, you invalidate them and lead them to feel like they are unworthy of having their own opinion and feelings on the matter. Furthermore, you make it seem as though your way is the only right way and that they must agree with you or else a solution will never be reached. This type of totalitarian approach can result in hurt feelings, frustration, and feeling neglected and ignored by your spouse.

Instead, take the time to show respect to your partner's perspective. You can do this by giving them the opportunity to explain it, by listening when they speak, and by not interrupting them even if you disagree with them. If you have a rhetorical argument that you want to make, wait until they are completely done sharing their point before you share your case. That way, they feel respected even during a disagreement.

Remember, respect is the key to helping your partner feel safe, safety is the key to building trust, and trust is the key to having intimacy between you and your partner. Without respect, there is no safety, trust, or intimacy. You absolutely must respect your partner. When your partner trusts that they can disagree with you and have their own perspective without you resorting to treating them with disrespect, this proves that you are respecting their right to their own opinion.

Respecting your partner and their opinion will also help you hear each other out which can support you in finding common ground in your arguments. When this happens, it becomes easier for you to find a resolution because you are both in agreement on at least a few things. This means that you can find a common ground and meet in the middle to come up with a solution that serves both of you. As a result, you both end the argument feeling closure. This ensures that the argument is brought to a complete close and that you can both move on from the argument without feeling residual resentment or anger toward the other partner.

Be Honest About How You Feel

Whenever you experience a disagreement with your partner, it is essential that you stay transparent about how you are feeling. When you argue with someone, it can be easy to feel a difficulty in expressing your emotions. You might fear that your emotions will not be understood or accepted, or that your emotions will make you look weak. These types of fears can result in you holding back which ultimately end in your partner not knowing exactly where you are coming from.

Furthermore, if you are dishonest about your feelings, it can result in you feeling resentment toward your partner for not being more compassionate or considerate toward you. However, the primary reason why they are likely not showing empathy for your feelings is that you have not clearly or honestly expressed them.

Remember, in your relationship with your spouse it is acceptable and safe to be vulnerable. Being vulnerable and telling them your real feelings does not mean that you are weak or incapable. Instead, it proves that even in the challenging moments you trust them and the fact that they will show respect toward you and your feelings. If they do not, then you may need to consider alternative solutions than simply changing your communication as your problems may be deeper than misunderstandings or poor communicational skills.

If you are the type of person who struggles to identify their true feelings, ensure that you are clear about this with your partner. Be willing to admit that you do not yet know how you feel about something but that you want to take a few minutes to figure it out and then you will tell them. This helps you both communicate your needs and tell them the truth about your feelings. Then, it is easier for you to both be more understanding toward each other during your arguments.

Commit to Finding a Solution

Anytime you notice a conflict or disagreement arising between you and your partner, make the conscious commitment of finding a solution. When you stay focused on finding a solution, it is easier for you to fight fairly and stay compassionate. This is because you are not losing sight of your goal and falling into the habit of fighting for the need to be right or with the desire to hurt your partner in the way that you feel they are hurting you. Instead, you are focused on finding a way to communicate effectively so that you can both feel as though your conflict is resolved in your mutual interest.

During times where you are not experiencing conflict, you can let your partner know that this is your primary intention when a disagreement sparks. You can also invite them to share the same common goal with you. That way, anytime an argument breaks out between you, you can both trust that you are working toward the same goal during that argument. This will keep you both disagreeing with a positive focus, supporting you in ending any disagreements or fights in a way that is considerate toward both you and your partner.

Chapter 9: Couple communication. Love therapy.

Image 16: Free Credits

Maintain an active presence with your body language. Avoid fidgeting or looking over your shoulder like you're already mapping your way out. There should also be no scrolling on your phone. This can come across as plain disrespectful. Maintain comfortable eye contact. Such a posture will keep the conversation going.

What if you initiate small talk and the listener seems blank? Perhaps you're dealing with a conversation rookie who is still getting over social anxiety. Here, you have to speak some more of yourself to prod a response. Let's say you've met in a work seminar and you ask, 'Is this your first time here?' The person answers with a 'no', then awkward silence. You can add something more about yourself. 'Oh, I've been here before, although the speakers are different this year.' The person is then likely to ask about the previous year's speakers. There! You have a conversation going.

When communicating with others, there are three primary steps that occur - thought, encoding and decoding. If you're the sender, it starts from the information that resides in your mind or otherwise known as thoughts. Encoding happens if you decide to send the message to another person through words or other forms. Finally, decoding completes the process as the receiver translates the thoughts into something he or she understands.

Content is one and it refers to the actual words used when sending the message which is also known as language. The second element is context which refers to the way you delivered the message or otherwise referred as paralanguage. This element encompasses other key communication elements such as body language, gestures, eye expression, emotion and tone of voice.

Unfortunately, even though you've been communicating all your life, misunderstanding words and messages is a common occurrence of everyday life. Every person has different ways of interpreting words and context. You may think that you've communicated your ideas clearly but the receiver may not really fully grasp the importance or the full meaning of the message due to numerous communication barriers.

Anything that prevents you from conveying the message clearly and from the receiver understanding it correctly is considered a communication barrier. Barriers can be psychological or physical and the most common you'll probably face often include differences in culture, background, perception, bias, environment, noise and stress. In some instances, the message itself can be a barrier too especially if the focus is on the facts rather than the idea or message being transmitted.

Since most barriers are external and inherent to the receiver, communicating effectively is a tough feat to take on. Even so, it is one endeavor worth your effort. The key is to focus not on yourself but on the person or people you are trying to communicate to. Forget about being defensive, your ego or the need to feel superior if you truly want to be an effective communicator. Only by aspiring and training yourself to overcome communication barriers will you truly unleash the power of effective communication to every aspect of your life.

- Facilitate communication

-

Part of tuning into yourself and laying a strong foundation for good communication is figuring out your communication style **and** your love language. You will better understand yourself and your interactions with others, especially your partner. In this chapter, we'll go over the four communication styles; whether they manifest as passive, aggressive, passive-aggressive, or assertive; and how to identify your love language.

The communication styles

Everyone has a communication style. If you research them at all, you'll see that people have lots of different ideas and theories, and they're all probably right to some extent. To make it as clear as possible, we're going with four main styles, and then four "flavors," or ways that a person's style manifests and is expressed to others. The main styles come from Mark Murphy, a leadership coach. While these are often applied to communication in the workplace, we think they make sense in relationships, too. The styles are:

Analytical

People with an analytical style of communication aren't interested in small details or emotional asides. They like the facts. When listening to their partner tell a story or describe something, an analytical person can appear to be unemotional, but it's more about wanting to get the most essential information before they respond. Once they believe they have that information, they might rush their partner emotionally, and fail to understand the more complex side of things. They often need to be reminded to wait, listen, and pay closer attention to emotions instead of just the facts.

Intuitive

Like the analytical style, intuitive people don't need a lot of details. They are big-picture people. They go with their gut. In a relationship, a person with this style might respond or interrupt before their partner is done talking. This can appear rude, but that isn't their intention. They just believe they have all the information they need. An intuitive who sticks with "their gut" might also have trouble compromising, because they truly feel that they are right. The partner of someone with this style should be sure to communicate that they want them to listen and be open-minded.

Functional

These people **love** details. They want as much information as possible and will hesitate making a decision or responding if they don't feel informed. In a relationship, this can look like procrastinating. A person with a functional communication style may take a while to respond or express an emotion, because they're gathering information. They might ask their partner a lot of questions, and it might appear that they are "grilling" them. The partner of someone with functional communication should remember that they might need time, and that asking questions doesn't mean they aren't supportive.

Personal

Someone with a personal communication style is all about emotions and human connection. They really want to know about the feelings and thoughts behind the facts, and naturally express their own. In a relationship, this style can help build trust and vulnerability very quickly, but if the other person isn't as comfortable, it can cause some tension. Someone with a personal style should remember that not everybody shares their desire for emotional expression, and they should be wary of pushing someone's boundaries.

- Get past discussions on major issues

We already know what to do to solve certain issues but sometimes it is not that simple, because your spouse might think and act different, or as seen in some cases, your spouse might be the complete opposite of you. Because in love anything can happen, you are always going to see different cases, and it's only normal to have cases where the couple disagrees. Disagreements are not always that terrible as they sound, and often the solution is very simple. It's just a matter of finding a balance. In an ideal world, there would be no problem and everything will be smooth and simple; however, this is not the reality. In real life, even couples who are very similar in personality and have the same interests disagree with something. After all, we are not replicas of each other, and how boring will life be if everything and everybody were the same, right?

There are different reasons why couples disagree. Some are more serious than others. We can disagree on something as simple as in what show to watch tonight or what to cook for dinner. These things might seem innocent and not that important, but when they start happening, often they can start to turn into an issue. In other cases, however, an argument might be something more serious, such as an important financial decision, or one couple doing something that can affect the relationship and having complete disregard for the consequences. Every reason, whether small, simple, or big and serious ones are to be paid attention to. As always, the most important thing is to hear both parties. No matter how bad we want something, if others are also taking part in the decision-making or it affects others, we need to take them into consideration. We can't just have things our own way, particularly when it comes to relationships. As we learned in the previous chapter, couples need to do things together. One of the things that often needs to be addressed but somehow gets swept under the rug is marital sexual issues and even worse, some couples don't know or might not be able to recognize that they are having sexual problems in their relationships. We are now going to look at the signs.

Your marital sex life is being affected if:

• Your marriage is experiencing a lack of sex or sex between you is basically nonexistent.

• One or the two parties involved are no longer excited at the idea of being sexually intimate with each other.

- One or the two parties involved are not enjoying the sexual experience, and there are problems reaching climax.

- Your sex drives are completely different and this affects your emotional and sexual life.

- One of the partners feels like sex is a form of validation, and feels pressured to have sex.

- You and your partner never speak about sex. It is taboo.

Does anything on that list sound familiar? If so, do not be ashamed. It happens more often that you can imagine, and you are not the first or last couple to experience any of these. Now that we know what the problem might be, let's try to focus on possible solutions.

Conclusion

As you have learned, clear and effective communication is an essential piece of the foundation that all relationships need to thrive and survive. In a world where many opt to talk to their loved ones using some sort of device, isn't the time now to get back to the basics of communication and polish up our skills to ensure that our relationships are not left to rot at their core.

I hope that you have discovered some methods that you think will work wonders for you and your partner. Everyone could use a little tweaking when it comes to redefining the communication barriers in relationships. No couple deserves to have to climb over the tall walls we build around ourselves. Communication is the one thing that can break down impassable walls and bring two people closer together.

I challenge you to take at least one thing away from what you have read and start applying it today to begin the process of bettering your relationship. The best part is, you could use many of the techniques found in this book to better communication within your non-romantic relationships in life as well!

So, what are you waiting for? The only thing standing between you and a better relationship is finding the motivation to take action and start using the strategies you have acquired!

Did you find this book to be valuable and of use to you in any way? If so, please take a moment to leave me a review on Amazon. It is always appreciated! I wish you the best of luck in rediscovering why you fell in love with your partner through the avenues of effective communication.

Made in the USA
Monee, IL
20 January 2021